1

Lang Fafa Dampha

Sub-Saharan Africa and the
Bretton Woods Institutions

By the same author

1) Nationalism and Reparation in West Africa, L'Harmattan, April 2013.
2) *Afrique subsaharienne : mémoire, histoire et réparation*, L'Harmattan, June 2013.
3) Reparation for Slavery and Colonialism: the Teachings of Durban, CreateSpace, March 2015.
4) Alien Attitude (novel), CreateSpace, July 2015.
5) African Migrants (novel), CreateSpace, August 2015.
6) The United Nations and Sub-Saharan African Reparation, CreateSpace, August 2015.

The ideas and intentions behind the creation of the international economic institutions were good ones, yet they gradually evolved over the years to become something different.

Joseph Stiglitz, *Globalisation and its discontent*

3

Table of Contents

Introduction

The devastating consequences of World War II, that engendered both economic and political insecurity in the world, led to the establishment of the United Nations Organisation in San Francisco in 1945. The American village of Bretton Woods in New Hampshire also became the birthplace of the global financial and trade institutions. The agreements signed on July 22, 1944, called "Bretton Woods Agreements" paved the way to the post-war financial system and international trade. The main objective of this agreement was to establish the foundations of a global monetary policy, while promoting reconstruction and economic development in the countries affected by World War II. The creation of a monetary system capable of supporting post-war reconstruction was therefore at the centre of the Bretton Woods Agreement. However the pioneers of the agreement under the leadership of the United States also wanted to contain the spread of Communism in Europe. Like those of the United Nations, the decisions taken by the 44 States present at the signing of these agreements were against the Axis countries: Germany and Japan mainly. The Bretton Woods Agreement gave birth to three inter-governmental institutions, namely, the International Monetary Fund (IMF), the World Bank, and the General Agreement on Tariffs and Trade (GATT), transformed to the World Trade Organisation (WTO) in 1995.

Thanks to the dynamism of two renowned economists, John Maynard Keynes of the United Kingdom and Harry Dexter White of the United States of America, the agreements led to the decision to abandon the gold standard in force since World War I in favour of the gold exchange standard. The new system chose the dollar as the main currency at the expense of the Pound Sterling, which had been the principal currency before the agreements. From then on the prices of other currencies were pegged to the dollar, and the reserves of the central banks were no longer to be in gold, but in currencies. After an interim period of painfully maintaining fixed parities, the United States unilaterally abandoned the convertibility of the dollar into gold on 15 August 1971. The system of floating exchange rates was thence established on March 19, 1973, leading to the Jamaica Accord,[1] made at the meeting that took place in Kingston, Jamaica in January 1976. Its purpose was to revise the IMF's Articles of Agreement to reflect the new realities of floating exchange rates. The Interim Committee of the IMF consequently put a definitive end to the monetary system of fixed but adjustable exchange rates.

The World Trade Organisation (WTO) deals with the rules governing international trade. It was established on January 1, 1995, but the trading system that it represents dates to 1947, when GATT established the system on which the principles of the WTO are based. GATT was originally created as part of a broader plan for economic recovery after World War

---

[1] A global agreement, concluded in 1976 that ratified the end of the Bretton Woods System by allowing the price of gold to float with respect to the U.S. dollar. An amendment to the agreement in 1978 allowed for the creation of Special Drawing Right, which is a form of international reserve assets, created by the International Monetary Fund (IMF) in 1967, whose value is based on a portfolio of widely used currencies.

II. It was negotiated during the United Nations Conference on Trade and Employment (UNCTE) in Havana, Cuba, in November 1947, and was the outcome of the failure of negotiation to create the International Trade Organisation (ITO) to complement the International Monetary Fund and the World Bank. Its principal purpose was to reduce barriers to international trade, through the reduction of tariff barriers, subsidies on trade and quantitative restrictions through a series of agreements. But because it was not ratified, GATT remained a simple agreement, and not originally an organisation in the normal sense.

According to Article III of the WTO Agreements, its objectives are to:

> ...promote World Trade in a manner that benefits every country;[...]ensure that developing countries secure a better balance in the sharing of the advantages resulting from the expansion of international trade corresponding to their developmental needs; [...] demolish all hurdles to an open world trading system and usher in international economic renaissance because the world trade is an effective instrument to foster economic growth; [...] enhance competitiveness among all trading partners so as to benefit consumers and help in global integration; [...] increase the level of production and productivity with a view to ensuring the level of employment in the world; [...] expand and utilise world resources to the best; [...] improve the level of living for the global population and speed up economic development of the member nations.

This initiative geared towards regulating international trade led to a first series of agreements through the

GATT. However the pioneer States were unable to agree on its exact definition, and thereafter created a series of cycles of negotiations. The end of the Uruguay Round in January 1995 transformed the GATT to the WTO. Since it is not a United Nations specialised institution, it has only maintained close ties with the UN and its agencies. The relations of the two institutions are governed by the "Arrangements for Effective Cooperations-Relations between the WTO and the United Nations" signed on 15 November 1995. The Director General of the WTO participates on the Chief Executive Board which is the organ of coordination within the UN system.

According to its Articles of Agreement, the IMF is an inter-governmental financial organisation established to:

> ...promote international monetary cooperation, [...] exchange stability, maintain orderly exchange arrangements among members; [...] assist in the establishment of a multilateral system of payments in respect of current transactions between members and in the elimination of foreign exchange restrictions which hamper the growth of world trade; [...] give confidence to members by making the general resources of the Fund temporarily available to them under adequate safeguards, thus providing them with opportunity to correct maladjustments in their balance of payments without resorting to measures destructive of national or international prosperity; [...] shorten the duration and lessen the degree of disequilibrium in the international balances of payments of members. (Article 1)

It therefore plays the role of monitoring the world's financial system on the one hand, and that of prevention and relief of the global economic system on the other, which makes it a financial institution in its own right, with the mission of temporarily assisting countries with serious economic difficulties under the conditions of "sufficient guarantees." It is hence the last resort in the framework of liquidity in the international financial system, which avoids blocking trade and problems of solvency of a country or its central bank. This feature also attributes it the status of the central bank of central banks. Therefore apart from its core task of monitoring, preventing and ensuring relief of the international financial system, the Fund provides loans to countries whose treasuries and banking systems are in difficulty. This task distinguishes the IMF from the World Bank, which provides investment loans to Member States.

The World Bank Group today consists of five institutions, namely, the International Bank for Reconstruction and Development (IBRD[2], the International Finance Corporation (IFC)[3], The International Development Association (IDA)[4], the International Centre for Settlement of Investment Disputes (ICSID[5], and the Multilateral Investment Guarantee Agency (MIGA)[6].

---

[2]The International Bank for Reconstruction and Development (IBRD) is the original institution of the World Bank Group, established in 1944.

[3]The International Finance Corporation (IFC), established in 1956, is the lending arm of the World Bank Group in the private sector; it provides financial services to businesses investing in developing countries.

[4]The International Development Association (IDA), established in 1960, offers concessional loans and grants to developing countries.

[5]The International Centre for Settlement of Investment Disputes (ICSID) was

As we have indicated, the International Bank for Reconstruction and Development (IBRD) was primarily established to help countries affected by World War II in their post-war reconstruction and development efforts. Certain countries were adversely affected by the war, principally France, the United Kingdom, Germany and Japan; therefore they were the most concerned by the activities of the Bank, even if it now operates mostly in developing countries. This shows that the promotion of development in developing countries was secondary in the activities of the World Bank. Initially then, it financed major post-war reconstruction projects in the war-affected zones, mostly in Europe, and when these countries recovered socio-economically, the Bank oriented its activities towards the promotion of development in developing countries, and later also to countries that emerged from the disintegration of the Soviet Union.

Thus in spite of the fact that the World Bank is serving the entire world now, initially it was purely aimed at redressing the socio-economic problems of the West, when Africa was of little importance. It was after the improvement of the political and economic situations in the war-affected West, and the decolonisation of Africa and then the collapse of the Soviet Union, that its attention finally turned towards developing countries.

---

established in 1966 and provides international facilities for conciliation and arbitration of investment disputes.

[6]The Multilateral Investment Guarantee Agency (MIGA), established in 1988, promotes foreign investment by providing investors and lenders with guarantees against losses associated with non-commercial risks in developing countries. (worldbank.org)

What is the relationship between Sub-Saharan Africa and the Bretton Woods institutions? What are the roles of these institutions in African reconstruction? [7]

---

[7] Reconstruction, reparation and development are interchangeably used in this work.

The Bretton Woods institutions and African reconstruction

We have indicated that the agreements signed in July 1944 in Bretton Woods, New Hampshire, in the United States of America redefined the rules of global finance and commerce, and laid the basis of the international financial system of post-World War II, up to the time when the system reached its limits in 1971. The objective of the Bretton Woods conference that made the agreements was to establish a new global monetary organisation and promote reconstruction and economic development in the countries affected by World War II. We have also seen that the agreements created two institutions: the International Bank for Reconstruction and Development (IBRD), which with the International Development Association (IDA) is now called the World Bank (WB), and the International Monetary Fund (IMF). Originally, the IMF was created to help stabilise the international monetary and financial system, by offering credit, financial and technical assistance to countries experiencing balance of payment difficulties and/or financial and economic crises, under certain conditions. The World Bank, on the other hand, was established to help rebuild European economies devastated by World War II, but has now extended its operations to developing countries. A third body, which is our first subject in this chapter, was established to oversee the rules of international trade by supervising trade agreements and settling trade disputes. It was initiated as the General Agreement on Tariffs and Trade, made in 1948 and formally transformed in 1995 to the World Trade Organisation (WTO).

What is the relation between the Bretton Woods institutions and Africa in terms of African reconstruction?

The World Trade Organisation

We have underlined the idea that all societies are involved in the process of socio-economic progress, and that development is primarily linked to the factors of production of goods and services in a normal condition of freedom, peace and security. Also, it is the system of production and distribution that creates goods, services and hence jobs to improve living condition. No country can operate in autarky, by relying solely on national products. This means that each country is obliged to participate in international trade, to sell its products and services so as to acquire the goods and services it does not have, or even the goods and services it can produce, but over the production of which it has no comparative advantages.

When Africa was colonised, its raw materials, finished goods and system of production in general were controlled by the colonialists, mainly the United Kingdom, France and Portugal. Now that the colonisation of Africa has ended, if Britain and France want to acquire African products, they must do it through trade. It is the World Trade Organisation (WTO), an inter-governmental organisation, which takes care of international trade by establishing the rules governing trade between its Member States. Its aims are to increase international trade by promoting lower trade barriers and serving as a platform for negotiation and settling disputes on trade matters; to raise standards of living by ensuring full employment and full use of global resources, and the increase of production and exchange of goods and services.

We have seen that the former GATT was not a real organisation, but simply a multilateral and legal arrangement to regulate international trade. The WTO that succeeded it was set up as a permanent body to regulate trade in goods and services, intellectual property rights, foreign investment, etc. Therefore the GATT laid the foundation for the operation of the WTO, but the latter incorporates several features that the GATT did not have. The most outstanding of these is the global trade in services like telecommunication and banking, which have now become the fastest growing sectors of the international economy, representing approximately two-thirds of the global production.

At the heart of the World Trade Organisation are found the agreements negotiated and signed in Marrakesh by the founding countries, and ratified by their parliaments.[8] Within the World Trade Organisation there are members and observers, which can be States as well as international organisations like the United Nations, the World Bank, the International Monetary Fund (IMF) etc. Apart from the Holy See (Vatican) government, observer governments must engage in accession negotiations within five years of becoming observers. The observer status for inter-governmental organisations in the World Trade

---

[8]The Governments of the Commonwealth of Australia, the Kingdom of Belgium, Brazil, Burma, Canada, Ceylon, the Republic of Chile, the Republic of China, the Republic of Cuba, the Czechoslovak Republic, the French Republic, India, Lebanon, the Grand-Duchy of Luxembourg, the Kingdom of the Netherlands, New Zealand, the Kingdom of Norway, Pakistan, Southern Rhodesia, Syria, the Union of South Africa, the United Kingdom of Great Britain and Northern Ireland, and the United States of America (Preamble, GATT 1947)

Organisation allows them to follow trade discussions and negotiations on matters and domains of direct interest to them. (wto.org)

The World Trade Organisation has a pyramidal structure with four levels:

i. The Ministerial Conference, which is the supreme authority and structure, composed of representatives of all Member States. It is held at least once every two years, and has the competence and authority to make decisions on trade agreements.

ii. The General Council is the World Trade Organisation's highest-level decision-making body in Geneva; like the Ministerial Conference, it is composed of representatives (usually ambassadors or their equivalents) from all Member States. It meets in two forms: as a dispute settlement body and as a body of trade policy review of Member States, and has the authority to act on behalf of the ministerial conference.

iii. The Council for Trade in Goods (Goods Council), oversees the implementation of all agreements relating to trade in goods, even though many of the WTO agreements provide for their own supervisory bodies. It consists of 10 committees dealing with specific issues, such as market access, agriculture, anti-dumping measures, subsidies... The committees consist of all Member States. A working party on state trading enterprises and the Information Technology Agreement (ITA) committee also report to the Goods Council.

iv. Other committees at different levels, in which representatives of all members can participate. (wto.org)

These last two bodies act under the General Council. The Secretariat of the World Trade Organisation is in Geneva, under the authority of a Director General nominated by the Ministerial Conference. It has no initiative role or capacity and exercises only ceremonial and diplomatic functions, unlike the Secretary General of the United Nations Organisation. We have said that the World Trade Organisation is essentially a place of negotiation, where all the governments of the Member States work together to resolve trade disputes and facilitate agreements and procedures. It has a jurisdictional competence, and through its General Council, one country can file a complaint against another.

Several agreements within the World Trade Organisation govern the totality of the domains related to trade as follows:

i. General Agreement on Tariffs and Trade (GATT), still in force but the WTO now incorporates its provisions, and refers to this version of the General Agreement as GATT 1994, which is distinct from the General Agreement in force since 1948, referred to as GATT 1947, the founding pillar of the WTO. However, the provisions of the WTO take precedence over GATT 1994;

ii. Agreement on Agriculture (AoA);

iii. General Agreement on Trade in Services (GATS);

iv. The Agreement on Trade-Related Investment Measures (TRIMS);

v. Agreement on Trade-Related Aspects of Intellectual Property Rights (TRIPS);

vi.   Agreement on Technical Barriers to Trade (TBT);

vii. Agreement on Sanitary and Phytosanitary Measures - (SPS).

As it is essentially a place for settlement of trade disputes, its operations are largely based on negotiations such as the Uruguay Round, held from 1986 to 1994, which were the previous negotiations conducted within the framework of the General Agreement on Tariffs and Trade (GATT), and the Doha Development Agenda launched in 2001, representing the current World Trade negotiations, which has now been extended to the Bali Agreement of December 2013.

The general idea of the GATT and then the World Trade Organisation has mainly been based on neo-liberal thinking, a reflection on the theory of "comparative advantages" advanced by the British economist David Ricardo in the 19th century. According to Ricardo, each country should specialise in the production of the goods it can produce at a relatively lower cost. Using the wine and cloth trade between England and Portugal as an example, he demonstrated that each nation, even the least competitive, has an interest (in perfect competition, without socio-political influence), in participating in international trade by specialising in the production of goods and services in which they have a relative disadvantage with the least negative consequences or the greatest relative advantage. For example, Portugal, in a given number of hours of labour, produced 20 metres of cloth and 300 litres of wine while England with the same number of hours comparatively produced 10 metres of cloth and 100 litres of wine. England was therefore at a disadvantage in the two sectors of production.

In the context of free trade[9] and according to Ricardo's theory, it would be more beneficial for England to specialise in producing cloth, in which it had a relative advantage, because for 10 metres of cloth, it would obtain 150 litres of Portuguese wine against 100 at home. Portugal would also gain more in specialising in the production of wine since trading with England 300 litres of Portuguese wine could obtain 30 metres of English cloth instead of 20 metres of Portuguese cloth. In other words, in the production of cloth, Portugal had an absolute advantage whereas England has a comparative advantage. The Portuguese could therefore acquire cloth exported by British producers, while the British acquired the Porto wine sold by Portuguese producers, cheaper.

If the policy of the World Trade Organisation is based on globalisation characterised by free trade, what is the fate of African reparation in that process? According to its Agreement, the World Trade Organisation promotes fair trade in order to facilitate and support socio-economic development for the well-being of all. What happens, then, between Africa and the West within the World Trade Organisation? What role does the World Trade Organisation play in African reparation? To answer these questions, we have to study the WTO's Agreement on Trade-Related Aspects of

---

[9] The Canadian government qualifies free trade as the exchange of goods and services between countries, regions or sub-regions without the imposition of tariffs, quotas or other restrictions; and under a normal atmosphere of perfect competition; productivity and living standards are usually higher under free trade. (canadianeconomy.gc.ca)

Intellectual Property Rights (TRIPS) and its Agreement on Agriculture (AoA) in the context of the Doha Development Agenda and the recent Bali Agreement made in December, 2013, as well as the structure and functioning of the organisation.

The Doha Development Agenda and the Bali Agreement

The Doha Development Agenda (DDA), which began with the WTO Ministerial meeting in Doha, Qatar in 2001, is the first multilateral trade negotiation under the auspices of the World Trade Organisation. It aims at reducing trade barriers and hence augmenting and facilitating international trade, and was therefore a real opportunity for developing countries to prosper through international trade. Other ministerial meetings on the Doha Development Agenda followed in 2003 in Cancun, Mexico and in 2005 in Hong Kong. Negotiations were also carried out in Paris, France in 2005, Geneva in 2004, 2006, and 2008, and in Potsdam, Germany in 2007.

However, discussions on the DDA have been marred by differences on major issues like industrial tariffs and non-tariff barriers, agriculture, services and trade remedies, especially between the European Union, the United States and Japan at one end and developing countries led by Brazil, China, India, South Africa, South Korea at the other end. There has been strong protest against agricultural subsidies of the European Union, the United States of America and Japan to their farmers.

Negotiation on the Doha Development Agenda deteriorated drastically during the July 2008 meeting and had become an almost lost cause, leading to a failure to reach compromise especially on rules concerning agricultural import. African and other developing countries continued protesting against subsidies by the West to their farmers. In April 2011, the WTO through its Director General at the time, Mr Pascal Lamy[10], although indicating that "the picture is impressive in the significant progress achieved so far," expressed concern about "the remaining divides," and asked Member States to "think hard about the consequences of throwing away ten years of solid multilateral work," calling on them to "use the upcoming weeks to talk to each other and build bridges." (wto.org) Although no significant progress was made from the April 2011 negotiations, trade negotiations were not jeopardised.

Negotiations on the Doha Development Agenda failed for several reasons, but the main one is the huge difference between the developed and developing worlds over almost all areas. The agricultural proposals of mainly EU and USA on the one hand and the G20[11] developing countries on the other, were strikingly different. Developing countries are very much concerned about the protective agricultural policies and trading practices of Japan, the European Union and the United States. Farm subsidies of the European Union in their Common Agricultural Policy[12] and the United States agricultural subsidies were major aspects of contestation. Notwithstanding its relatively small and declining share in world trade, agriculture has been a

---

[10] Pascal Lamy (a French citizen) was Director General of the World Trade Organisation from 1 September 2005 to 1 September 2013.

[11] The G20, also known as the Group of 20 (and, occasionally, the G21, G23 or G20+) is a bloc of developing nations established on 20 August 2003. Distinct and separate from the G-20 major economies, the group emerged at the 5th Ministerial WTO conference, held in Cancun, Mexico, from 10 September to 14 September 2003.

[12] The Common Agricultural Policy (CAP) of the European Union supports European farmers by providing direct payments, price guarantees, and other supports, including quotas and tariffs on some imported produce. The policy is run on a pan-European basis, meaning that national governments cannot provide direct aid to their farmers; the funds are administered via the CAP.

major contention in international trade negotiations, causing a lot of problems in the Uruguay Round in the late 1980s and early 1990s, and has been the major bottleneck in the Doha multilateral trade negotiations, consequently causing substantial failures in the Cancun Ministerial Meeting on the DDA, in September 2003. Globally, agriculture is relatively less relevant in the world economy but hugely important for developing countries, most of whose economies rely heavily on agricultural products. The relative unimportance of agriculture in the global economy has motivated some groups, notably from the West, to suggest its side-lining in trade negotiations as in the GATT prior to the Uruguay Round. However, putting aside agriculture especially concerning the DDA would be damaging to developing countries, simply because agricultural production, as we have identified, is very important to them. It hence took about nine months to reach a consensus on the Doha work programme, commonly referred to as the July Framework Agreement, (WTO 2004).

Developing countries in their relations with the developed countries have now finally had the confidence to effectively stand against situations that were unfavourable to them, as symbolised by the G20 developing countries as a trade bloc. However the negotiation of the G20 developing nations led by the G4, namely Brazil, China, India and South Africa in the name of all the developing countries, has not had much impact on the influence and capacity of the developing countries collectively, especially in Sub-Saharan Africa in trade proposals.

The Doha Development Agenda is worth fighting for because its success would tend to enhance the world economy and boost the prospects for cooperation in critical domains like the environment. A successful DDA will equally create greater economic opportunities for developing countries as a result of improved market access, the implementation of the "duty free and quota free" proposal, lowering "red tape"[13] and significant reductions in tariff escalation (tariff peaks). It will ensure tariff and subsidy cuts for workers and farmers in developing countries, and increase the volume of international trade and global income. The Doha deal as proposed, if effectively administered, would also certainly go beyond the primary benefit of additional market access gains, to serve as a deterrent for governments to adopt protectionist policies. Doha is also believed to be able to serve the environment by reducing environmental pollution and destruction caused by agricultural and other production programmes. Globally then it could increase job opportunities, especially in the developing world and promote sustainable and greener growth.

However, the protection of agricultural products, as we have indicated, has bitterly divided the G20 developing countries and the West. Under the Doha Development Agenda, the Uruguay Round Agreement on Agriculture had to be renegotiated, but it led to no positive results, because the European Union and the United States have been unwilling to change their positions of offering subsidies to their farmers.

---

[13] Reducing the cost and delays involved in international trade at borders, in ports and in transit.

During the final stages of negotiation in the ninth World Trade Organisation Ministerial Conference held in Bali, Indonesia, in December, 2013, Kofi Annan, former Secretary General of the United Nations Organisation and Chair of the Africa Progress Panel at the meeting, urged all the participants to reach an agreement on trade enhancement arguing that:

> A deal on trade facilitation should be a low-hanging fruit to benefit millions of people all around the world. By cutting red tape and boosting access to critical trade information, for example, such a deal would reduce the costs of trade between countries, help small traders get their goods to markets and improve transparency and good governance. This is especially important for Africa with its 54 nations – several of them landlocked – where the current, complicated procedures of transporting goods across borders increase costs, reduce productivity and hinder regional trade [...] such a deal is the best hope we have for keeping global trade discussions alive. If we do not get a deal in Bali, then we face the risk that rich countries focus on trade deals between themselves, thereby excluding lower income countries who need this trade the most. (africaprogresspanel.org)

Here Kofi Annan is expressing the fear that disagreement would lead to the predominance of bilateral trade agreements especially by the West, which would be to the detriment of developing countries. Indeed Trade Ministers from 159 Member States of the World Trade Organisation have reached a deal to enhance global trade. It is the first comprehensive agreement of the WTO since it was founded in 1995, intending to generally simplify trade procedures across the borders, including the improvement of duty-free access for goods sold by developing countries. Accordingly the Bali agreement could generate between $400 billion and $1 trillion in world trade, and would render developing countries more room to increase farm subsidies. This has motivated the new World Trade Organisation Director General, Roberto Azevedo, to declare: "...For the first time in our history, the WTO has truly delivered. [...] This time the entire membership came together. We have put the 'world' back in World Trade Organisation." For the British Prime Minister, David Cameron, "...the 'historic' agreement could be a 'lifeline' for the world's poorest people, as well as benefiting British businesses to the tune of more than $1bn (£600m)." (bbc.co.uk) The Bali agreement is thus expected to benefit all the Member States of the WTO. The simple act of reaching the first comprehensive agreement since the transformation of the General Agreement on Tariffs and Trade to the World Trade Organisation, after decades of protracted trade negotiations, could motivate us to acclaim the Bali deal. It has however been criticised by development campaigners for not going far enough. Has the Bali deal marginalised the interest of the African continent? What is its essence to African reparation?

According to Africa Trade Network:

The agreed text on trade facilitation is the very opposite of what African countries need to address the fundamental and peculiar challenges that they face in moving goods and services across national borders. The text imposes obligations on all countries to adopt customs procedures which are standard in the advanced industrial countries, and which most of the big emerging economies have already voluntarily adopted, and which are commensurate with the stage of economic development. African countries on the other hand, have to undertake massive legislative, policy and infrastructural changes to live up to these standards. However, the prior understanding to provide commensurate policy, technical, institutional and financial space and support for African countries to meet these changes was not adequately addressed in the text. If anything, the even weaker commitments agreed at the start of the Bali meeting were diluted even further – e.g. references to financial support have been removed from the text. Furthermore, the new binding rules adopted take away even the means by which African countries can mobilise their own resources to meet these new changes. Above all, rather than simplify customs procedures, the text introduces new processes which stand to give foreign corporations undue influence in the customs of African countries and diminish the role of domestic customs operators, further undermining African agenda of boosting intra-African trade and regional integration. (trademarksa.org)

This argument accused the Bali deal of being based on "customs procedures" which already exist in the developed world, and hence coerced developing countries to undergo legislative, policy and infrastructural transformations to be in line with the procedures. Also, earlier commitments and support that are beneficial to intra-African trade were not addressed by Bali; it has also been accused of trashing the means of developing countries to mobilise their own resources to meet the new challenges. The Bali Agreement, therefore, has the tendency to undermine intra-African trade and regional integration which are important pillars of African reparation.

The Bali deal in fact comprises three factors, namely trade facilitation, agriculture and boosting Least Developed Countries (LDC) trade. Trade facilitation as the name indicates refers to the simplification of trade by reducing the cost of trading at borders, which as we have seen is expected to save up to $1 trillion in the global economy, if Member States succeed in cutting the red tape. The agriculture and cotton package aims at finding a sustainable mechanism for developing countries to have more options for food security without other Member States challenging them at the WTO, and to create improved access to market for cotton producers from LDCs, as well as development assistance for producers in some countries. The LDC trade boosting package aims at improving market access and enhancing rules of origin[14] in developed countries.

To effectively examine the feasibility, appropriateness or relevance of the Bali Agreement to African reparation, we have to reflect on its nature and relate it to the previous trade negotiation, the Doha Development Agenda (DDA). We have seen that the DDA was an endeavoring agenda launched during the 4th Ministerial Conference in Doha, Qatar, in 2001, whose negotiations met with a lot of difficulties, because of the divergent interests of the negotiating parties. The history of WTO negotiations has shown

---

[14] Rules of origin are the criteria required to determine the national origin source of a product. The duties and restrictions in several cases depend on the source of imports.

that the Bali negotiations had to succeed not to jeopardise the relevance and role of the Organisation as the world's most viable trade negotiating body, especially in the face of the proliferation of bilateral trade agreements, as highlighted by Isabelle Ramdoo:

> The spectre of a failure in Bali was also simply not something many could afford to contemplate, [...] Parallel to the WTO, most developed countries are busy negotiating very ambitious trade agreements with their major trading partners, such as the US-EU Transatlantic Trade and Investment Partnership Agreement or the US Trans-Pacific Partnership Agreement, to name two major ones. [...] Stripping the WTO of its negotiating arm would have, therefore, implied that bilateral negotiating partners would have all the arguments and all the reasons to open the Pandora's box on sensitive issues. And this is too politically sensitive to let go.[...] It was clear that there was no politically acceptable alternative to the WTO as a negotiating body and that bilateral trade agreements, although strategically important to boost trade, have their limits in terms of what would be up for negotiation. (ecdpm-talkingpoints.org)

There had been a great deal of enthusiasm and optimism about the role of the DDA in addressing the imbalances in the global trading system, but it became constrained by intractable differences, which led most Member States to find alternative bilateral and regional trade agreements. The Bali Agreement therefore had to provide an enhancement to the multilateral trading system which had undergone enormous difficulties in the Doha Development Agenda, and whose negotiations on agriculture were based on two main aspects. First, the opening of the world market to all agricultural products, including substantial improvements in market access to agricultural products until all the barriers are lifted. Second, the reduction of all forms of export subsidies in agriculture to 20 percent, and a reduction of support measures that can cause distortions in trade, in the perspective of their gradual elimination.

The provisions of the Bali agreement are liable to further weaken earlier commitments on trade facilitation and agriculture. For example negotiation on cotton has been Africa's simple test about equity of the multilateral trading system; however only consideration of further action on commitments already made has been promised in the Bali agreement. The same thing applies to other issues including rules of origin and duty-free quota-free market access for LDCs. Therefore instead of contesting the general inclination of the World Trade Organisation that relatively disregarded the concerns of LDCs, the Bali Agreement has added to more neo-liberal attitudes. All these symbolise the challenges facing Africa in globalisation vis-à-vis its reparation efforts. The Bali agreement also reduced the negotiations around agriculture to simple public stockholding programmes and tariff-rate quotas less than the range initially intended at in Doha, and which instigated the failure of previous talks.

In the Uruguay Round in 1994, developing countries had supposed that the opening of the market for agricultural goods, especially the markets in developed countries would enable them to benefit from their comparative advantages in certain agricultural products;

an idea that most likely motivated them to accept the agreement in which other aspects were disadvantageous to them, such as the Agreement on Trade and Intellectual Property. The Common Agricultural Policy (CAP) of the European Union was based on direct aid to European farmers. The United States and the European Union have made a joint proposal called "Framework for a common approach on agricultural issues,"[15] and adopted the same policy, even though the United States with other producers, including the Cairns Group[16] considered the reform of the policy of the European Union insufficient. According to strategically different methods, both the United States and the European Union had been supporting their farmers more than was recommended by the WTO Agreement on Agriculture. The United States, for example, "supports its farmers up to $46 billion in aid, according to estimates by the Organisation for Economic Cooperation and Development."(Insee.fr) Subsidies from the United States and the European Union to their farmers continued, despite protests by developing countries against them. These supports might have political implications in the United States and the European Union, but they enormously affect African farmers, especially the cotton farmers because they

---

[15] Cadre pour une approche commune sur des questions agricoles.

[16] The Cairns Group is a group of exporters of agricultural products, established in August 1986 in Cairns, Australia, who rallied in favour of trade liberalisation in this sector. There are 19 countries in the group representing a significant share of world agricultural exports: Australia, South Africa, Argentina, Brazil, Colombia, Costa Rica, Bolivia, Canada, Chile, Indonesia, Malaysia, Guatemala, New Zealand, Pakistan, Paraguay, Peru, Philippines, Thailand and Uruguay. The group is a kind of reaction against the persistent protectionism in the United States and the European Union, especially in the field of the Common Agricultural Policy.

triggered a fall in the price of agricultural products especially cotton on the world market, causing huge losses. The earnings of African cotton producers in Benin, Burkina Faso, Chad, The Gambia and Mali fell dramatically. In West Africa, for example, more than 10 million people depend on cotton and have no alternative means of survival. The irony is that the livelihood of millions of African farmers is threatened by just thirty thousand North American farmers. At the fifth World Trade Organisation Ministerial Conference in September 2003 in Cancun, a proposal was submitted by the four major African producers of cotton (Benin, Burkina Faso, Mali and Chad) for the total elimination of subsidies by the West, particularly the United States and the European Union. This group of four also claimed financial compensation for losses incurred by African farmers due to subsidies of the West to their farmers. The rejection of these claims angered the Least Developed Countries and the African, Caribbean and Pacific group of States (ACP). Hence for the second time, after the Seattle Ministerial Conference, a WTO Ministerial Conference ended without consensus. The Cancun summit in 2003 was marked by an alliance of developing countries against the proposed liberalisation of services, examined on the table. This alliance also sought a change in the agricultural policies of the developing countries, and resulted, given the refusal of these countries, in the failure of the negotiations.

Mary Robinson[17] urged the West to revise its protective policy of subsidy, in order to guarantee an

---

[17] Mary Robinson was born in 1944 in Ballina, County Mayo. She is the first woman President of Ireland (1990-1997), and former United Nations High Commissioner for Human Rights (1997-2002), also founder and President of

environment of fair trade, and ensure the normal life to which everyone is entitled. However, with the Doha Declaration as we have seen, the World Trade Organisation decided to systematically incorporate in every negotiation, "a special and differential treatment" to take into account the special needs of developing countries, which is a positive advancement.

Concerning agriculture, the Bali agreement has involved more flexibility vis-à-vis the existing rules on farm subsidies. Negotiations at Bali covered agricultural subsidies, but an agreement on these was postponed because of India's insistence on continuing to subsidise farm products as part of its "food security" programme, which is likely to obstruct the WTO rules that limit subsidies. A peace clause, as a compromise deal, under which members are not to initiate WTO disputes against those breaching the subsidy limits as part of a food-security programme, was agreed on for a period of four years, with the idea that a final settlement will be reached after that period. The Bali deal has therefore done little to reduce farm subsidies that have been seriously hurting African farmers, (this time it has been insisted on by India, a member of the G20 developing countries), because there is very little assurance that the expected final settlement will take place. This new peace clause is likely to protect or motivate mostly Western countries that have been subsidising cotton and other products for their farmers, and having benefited from an initial peace clause between 2001 and 2003, to continue their subsidy programmes

---

Realising Rights: The Ethical Globalisation Initiative (2002-2010). She is a human rights advocate.

Therefore, African countries that have been affected by the Euro-American subsidies will suffer more from the Bali peace clause. In fact the Bali Agreement has almost neglected issues that affect agriculture in Africa including subsidies that we have just seen, and dumping; because the negotiations on agriculture only generated a provisional device that will lead to supplementary negotiations in order to obtain an enduring solution, which is not certain. According to John Hilary of War on Want, a UK-based group: "The negotiations have failed to secure permanent protection for countries to safeguard the food rights of their peoples, exposing hundreds of millions to the prospect of hunger and starvation simply in order to satisfy the dogma of free trade." (bbc.co.uk) The Bali deal seeks further reductions in tariffs on industrial goods, farm subsidies and barriers to international trade in services. However agreement on the rest of the negotiations on the Doha Development Agenda is not guaranteed.

Concerning the special package for Least Developed Countries especially boosting trade, the Bali deal is basically on clauses with little functioning value, except perhaps for trade facilitation, which is the most important component of the agreement intending to "cut the red tape", by setting minimum standards for the administration of customs duties i.e. to smooth the flow of trade and for market access. According to Patrick Kanyimbo and Calvin Manduna:

Trade facilitation is vital for Africa's own competitiveness as it will reduce costs for traders. While tariffs have progressively fallen, the key challenge to intra-African trade is non-tariff barriers that stifle the movement of goods, services and people across borders. To use a clichéd example, it has often been said that shipping a car from Japan to Abidjan costs US $1,500, but shipping the same car from Abidjan to Addis Ababa costs US $5,000. There are 16 landlocked countries on the continent. For these countries, the average customs transaction involves 20 to 30 steps, 40 documents, 200 data elements and re-keying of 60 per cent to 70 per cent of all data at least once. It therefore comes as no surprise that trade facilitation bottlenecks such as border crossing procedures, cumbersome documentation, regulations and non-tariff barriers such as police checks account for 14 per cent of trade costs in Africa's landlocked countries, compared to a developing country average of 8.6 per cent. (afdb.org)

Africa has the longest customs delays in the world, for example 36 hours to get goods through the customs post at the Victoria Falls crossing from Zambia into Zimbabwe, according to the African Development Bank. (ibid) Also that there are generally more obstacles to negotiate once goods are over the border; the highway between Lagos and Abuja in Nigeria has 69 official checkpoints. (africaprogresspanel.org). There is evidence that this involves a big cost to trading in many parts of Sub-Saharan Africa, especially in the landlocked countries. Therefore, there would be a huge benefit from reducing trade barriers to African countries. However, the benefit from trade facilitation is less certain than tariff reduction or quotas from more traditional agreements, in part because it is not certain that governments will quickly implement the new standards; notwithstanding the fact that the Bali agreement is legally binding, which should under normal circumstances provide reassurance on its effective implementation.

The World Trade Organisation sets rules to protect intellectual property rights and its procedures for settling international trade disputes, which are normally binding on Member States. The Agreement on Trade-Related Aspects of Intellectual Property Rights (TRIPS), signed in Marrakesh in 1994 that concluded the Uruguay Round, protects copyrights, trademarks and patents, and sets the minimum standards of protection for the different categories of property rights, which accordingly should be incorporated and applied by Member States in accordance with the principles and provisions of the agreement. The objective of TRIPS is to bring the system of Intellectual Property Rights (IPR) globally under a common international standard of rules to solve the problems of international piracy and Intellectual Property Rights infringements. Under TRIPS, IPR extends for twenty (20) years from the date of filing the patent, including medications protected by these rights, even in their generic form. In the actual TRIPS agreement, "a number of provisions have become known as TRIPS public health safeguards because they enhance the affordability and availability of medicines. They are "compulsory licensing, extension of the transition period for the enforcement of intellectual property rights, parallel imports, allowing generic drugs producers to prepare production and obtain regulatory approval for generic versions of patent medicines before the patent expires - Bolar provision."[18] (who.int)

---

[18] Article 30 of TRIPs allows for limited exceptions to the rights conferred to the

Developing countries protested against TRIPS, because it limited their access to innovation and technological development that the agreement covered, even though they accepted it in the end. The philosophy of TRIPS is based on the transfer of know-how, particularly between developed and developing countries, and as we have just seen, the conditions of access to property rights supporting the notion of the protection of international patent is for a minimum of twenty (20) years covering the products, including medicinal drugs. It is obvious that patents encourage research and development in all sectors, in this case the pharmaceutical sector, but the restriction of technical information imposed by TRIPS reinforces the already existing inequalities between developed and developing countries. Indeed TRIPS established a balance between incentives for research and development and people's access to and use of existing inventions and creations. African countries are, however, condemned by this agreement to remain buyers of the products and not to acquire and implement the production techniques even in the case of serious health needs, which made TRIPS a major source of injustice, despite the fact that the least developed countries are allowed a longer transition period in which to comply with the provisions of the agreement. Intellectual Property Rights is justified from

---

patent holder. The exceptions however can be challenged and reviewed by the WTO. For pharmaceuticals, the most common exception to the exclusive rights of patent holders is mostly referred to as the 'Bolar provision', which refers to a court case in the US, *Roche Products Inc. vs. Bolar Pharmaceutical Co.* which dealt with the same type of exception. It allows (generic) manufacturers to produce test-batches of the product concerned before the patent expires, so as to collect the necessary data to submit to the authorities for registration; this is meant to reduce the delay for generic products to enter the market after the patent has expired, and thus to enhance competition.

the point of view of commercial law, but this one concerning medicinal drugs infringes the basic rights of access of all to medicine in the context of humanity, which is important for Africa and to the health needs of its population. TRIPS had huge implications for the production of and access to drugs, particularly in developing countries. The lawsuit against the Government of South Africa by thirty nine (39) pharmaceutical companies for having adopted the Medicines and Related Substances Control Amendment Act, No. 90 of 1997, a law on the control of drugs in the country, confirms the importance of this situation contrasting the right to health and commercial law. The Medicines and Related Substances Control Amendment Act authorised parallel importations and substitution or manufacture of medicine in South Africa and in certain circumstances to deal with the problem of HIV/AIDS. The pharmaceutical firms in their complaint leaned on the provisions of TRIPS, which protects the licensing of patented drugs, arguing that the law is unconstitutional because it substitutes the medicines of pharmaceutical laboratories with generics.

South Africa is a country in which 10% of the population, (about five million people) are affected by HIV/AIDS, the majority of whom cannot afford the treatment they need, and several other countries in Sub-Saharan Africa are in the same boat. Millions of Africans, according to the World Health Organisation (WHO), die each year because of lack of access to treatment. In the case of South Africa, concerning the problem of HIV/AIDS, the government decided to produce generic medicines, despite the filing of lawsuits by the multinational pharmaceutical companies. Two completely different factors collide here: public health and intellectual property; and it is logical that public health should come before profit, as Mr. Pascal Lamy proposed in 2005. However, it is the opposite that seemed to be happening. Yet paragraph 4 of the Doha Declaration on TRIPS and Public Health, made at the Doha Ministerial Conference in November 2001 states:

> ...We agree that the TRIPS Agreement does not and should not prevent members from taking measures to protect public health. Accordingly, while reiterating our commitment to the TRIPS Agreement, we affirm that the Agreement can and should be interpreted and implemented in a manner supportive of WTO members' right to protect public health and, in particular, to promote access to medicines for all. In this connection, we reaffirm the right of WTO members to use, to the full, the provisions in the TRIPS Agreement, which provide flexibility for this purpose. (worldtradelaw.net)

The pharmaceutical companies eventually withdrew their complaint in May 2001 mainly because of pressure from the Treatment Action Campaign - (TAC) in South Africa, that was gradually supported by other organisations such as Doctors Without Borders - *Médecins Sans Frontières* (MSF), Oxfam International, AIDS Law Project... Some Western politicians contributed to the struggle and the European parliament consequently supported the idea of access to cheap medicines. In April 2001, in an interview with the Observer newspaper, Gordon Brown, the then Chancellor of the Exchequer of Great Britain asked pharmaceutical firms to find a means of solving the problem. He proposed tax cuts on research and development. (medcost.fr) Nelson Mandela, in a televised speech asked the laboratories to change their methods. (ibid) The fact that pharmaceutical companies are no longer opposed to the use of "generics" of these drugs thanks partly to the pressure of these NGOs and those of some individual politicians is very positive even if it does not completely solve the problem of access to treatment.

On August 30, 2003 in Cancun, Member States reached an agreement after nearly nine months of negotiations, which allows the import of generic drugs for poor countries short of pharmaceutical industry. This agreement is a step forward, but several Non-Governmental Organisations denounced the complexity and difficulty of its implementation. (ladocumentationfrancaise.fr)

In the Doha Round, negotiations on non-agricultural products, which "include industrial products, manufactured goods, textiles, fuels and mining products, footwear, jewellery, forest products, fish and fish products, as well as chemicals," focus on reducing or eliminating tariffs, "including tariff peaks, high tariffs, tariff escalation and non-tariff barriers for non-agricultural goods, in particular on products of export interest to developing countries". (wto.org) Although there are flexibilities to enable developing countries to protect a limited percentage of their most sensitive sectors against the effect of a tariff reduction, as well as special treatment for small and vulnerable economies and Least Developed Countries, the proposal presented by the Chairman of the negotiating Group on July 17 was considered bad for developing countries. According to critics, the proposal on market access for non-agricultural products:

... Would lead to an average reduction in tariffs of about 60 percent for developing countries, which will bring the average tariff to 12 percent, such a level that it would undermine the prospects for industrial development in many developing countries. In addition, the flexibilities of the proposed tariff that should allow developing countries to protect and develop specific areas of intensive labour, such as textiles and clothing, leather and footwear, plastic, paper, rubber, metals, automotive and furniture are so small that they would not provide protection to a very low employment vulnerable workforce, which would further reduce development prospects.[19](imfmetal.org)

The functioning of the World Trade Organisation indicates that it is a democratic institution, since all the Member States decide by "consensus," each member having one vote. In this context, the smallest Member State can oppose and block a decision, even if powerful and rich countries like the United States and China are in favour of it. It is this situation that pushed Mr Mike Moore,[20] to reject the criticism based on the lack of

---

[19] ...conduirait à une réduction moyenne des tarifs douaniers d'environ 60 pour cent pour les pays en développement, ce qui porterait le niveau tarifaire moyen à 12 pour cent, un niveau si bas qu'il compromettrait les perspectives de développement industriel dans de nombreux pays en développement. En outre, les flexibilités tarifaires proposées qui devraient permettre aux pays en développement de protéger et développer des secteurs spécifiques à forte intensité de main-d'œuvre, comme le textile et l'habillement, le cuir et la chaussure, le plastique, le papier, le caoutchouc, les métaux, l'automobile et l'ameublement, sont si minimes qu'elles n'assureraient qu'une protection de l'emploi très faible à une main-d'œuvre vulnérable, ce qui ne ferait que réduire encore les perspectives de développement.

democracy within the World Trade Organisation. Does the World Trade Organisation function in a reasonably democratic way? In theory the answer is yes. It is true that each Member State has one vote, regardless of its economic, political or military strength or weakness. However, the presence in Geneva of an accredited ambassador for each Member State is considered a necessity for their normal participations. Yet several members of the World Trade Organisation, including many African countries could not afford to establish permanent representatives at the headquarters of the Organisation, in spite of the existence of programmes for capacity building and technical cooperation within the World Trade Organisation to promote the effective participation of developing countries in trade negotiations and in the commercial system in general. (wto.org) Some Member States have representatives in Geneva, but do not have the number of staff required to follow all the files under negotiation; and during WTO negotiations, the views of Member States that do not have representatives in Geneva are not taken into account. The consensus within the World Trade Organisation therefore concerns only those who attend the meetings, meaning that it is not the consent of the Organisation at large. The WTO should, in a cooperative and supportive manner, strengthen its capacity building programmes and technical cooperation to become more efficient and to assist and

---

[20]Michael Kenneth Moore, commonly known as Mike Moore, was born on 28 January 1949, in Whakatane, New Zealand. He is a New Zealand politician who has served as Prime Minister for a few months in 1990, and then Director-General of the World Trade Organisation. He is presently the New Zealand Ambassador to the United States.

allow countries that do not have the means to be represented in Geneva to participate and follow the negotiations.

In addition, the group of four, called the "Quad" that constitutes the Trade Ministers of the United States, Japan, Canada and the European Union, hold informal meetings in the office of the Director General, with some invited Member States, sometimes up to 30, to deal with preliminary negotiations, referred to as "the Green Room Meetings" whose conclusions are presented to other countries. If these Green Room Meetings are designed to serve as the basis for a consensus on critical issues under negotiation, and therefore as a factor of building common agreement within the Organisation, their representation selectively comes, apart from the Quad, from bigger and richer countries. In fact, the real decisions tend to be made during these meetings, just like the informal consultations of the United Nations Security Council. It would be interesting to know why the United States of America belongs to this group of four, and not The Gambia or Kenya. Why is the European Union part of it and not the African Union? In view of this, one can reasonably argue that there is no real democracy within the World Trade Organisation and its working methods hamper Africa's reparation efforts, at least in some way.

The general functioning of the World Trade Organisation indicates that it is a source of inequality, which confirms that reforming its functioning is crucial; and that there is clearly a double principle of equality amongst the Member States. If the World Trade Organisation is really committed to promoting economic development through trade, it must alongside endorse fair trade for all, especially developing countries, a good number of which are in Africa, still suffering from the negative effects of slavery and their colonial past. The Dispute Settlement Body[21] is presented as an important apparatus for developing countries, but its status is far from being jurisdictional. The violations of the principles and agreements, especially concerning subsidies by the United States, the European Union and Japan to their farmers, are very bad examples. The role of the Director General should also cease to be ceremonial and become more responsible, more independent and more engaged.

---

[21] The Dispute Settlement Body (DSB) of the World Trade Organisation (WTO) is a session of the General Council of the WTO, which is all the representatives of the WTO member governments, mostly at ambassadorial level, meeting together, responsible for making decisions on trade disputes between governments.

The International Monetary Fund and the World Bank.

In its Articles of Agreement, the International Monetary Fund is presented as a financial inter-governmental institution that plays the role of surveillance, prevention and protection of the global economic system; factors, which attribute to it the status of a financial institution in its own right. As for the World Bank, we have seen that it was created with the initial objective of helping Europe to recover from the effects of World War II. To attain this objective, it provided loans to countries in need.[22] We found that the African continent has depended on globalisation just like all other continents, but also on the legacy of its history.[23] What is the specific relationship of the International Monetary Fund and the World Bank to African reparation?

To understand the state of immediate post-colonial Sub-Saharan Africa, which propelled it to depend on its former colonisers and the Bretton Woods institutions for its development programmes in the post-colonial

---

[22] The Bank soon embarked on the preparation and execution of an important series of reconstruction loans to countries of Western Europe, the first of which was to France. The French loan application for $500 million arrived as a simple letter attached to an outline of the government's reconstruction program, the Monnet Plan. The overall requirements included $106 million for equipment, $180 million for coal and petroleum products, and $214 million for raw materials. The equipment included ships, freight cars, trucks, radio and electrical equipment, and coal mining equipment. The list of raw materials included fertilizers, copper, tin, synthetic rubber, animal fats and chemicals. (worldbank.org)

[23] Some African and Caribbean critics believed that the trans-Saharan and trans-Atlantic slave trades and Colonialism looted Africa to the point that it finds it difficult to get out of the abyss. See How Europe Underdeveloped Africa by Walter Rodney, and the Wretched of the Earth by Frantz Fanon.

epoch, it is important to understand the context of the political economy and international relations in which the continent evolved or grew during the period of Colonialism and immediate post-colonialism. During colonisation, the colonial masters introduced a production system in Africa purely based on commercial culture. For example, coffee and tea were strategically introduced in Kenya, groundnuts in The Gambia and Senegal; cocoa in Ghana, cotton in Angola etc. These products were intended for export to the metropolis, Paris, London, Lisbon... Thus, African countries during colonisation essentially specialised in growing one or two types of crops, rarely three, such as groundnut in Senegal and The Gambia. The growth of the economies of these countries was thus determined by the fluctuations in the prices of their commodities on the world market, which was the inevitable consequence of monoculture. During colonisation the majority of the African population were farmers; their prosperity or poverty, after independence, therefore depended directly on the prices of their products. Before the arrival of the colonial system the populations in The Gambia and Senegal, for example, were almost self-sufficient in the cultivation of their basic necessities such as rice and other products for local consumption, and many other regions of Africa were in the same category. Diversification by introducing cash crops for export in the production system, especially in the context of globalisation is good for the economy, but the colonial policy which almost coerced Africans to abandon the production of food crops necessary for the survival of the population to exclusively focus on the production of raw materials and other cash crops for export to the metropolis was done out of the context of constructive diversification, thereby causing a long-lasting negative impact on African economies whose legacy is still present.

Paradoxically, there is no link between industries in Africa and the products encouraged except mining, which are funded by the colonialists. In fact, the most harmful factor of this system for Africa is the total negligence of industrialisation by the colonial policy, which froze African industries that had existed in their own form before colonisation, especially in the West African region, which had to wait until the end of colonisation to begin germinating industries. In East and Southern Africa: Rhodesia, Kenya, South Africa, where the atmosphere is more favourable, the colonialists appropriated the land of the inhabitants and imposed on them a near-slave control, symbolised by the apartheid regime in Southern Africa.

The colonial policy of production, mainly geared towards cash crops for export, thus generated a huge lack of appropriate diversification and destroyed the local self-sufficiency in food crops in colonial economies in Africa. This monoculture oriented towards cash crops, not for local industries but for export characterised most countries in Sub-Saharan Africa, a phenomenon which adversely affected the post-colonial African economies.

According to Davison Budhoo, a former employee of the International Monetary Fund who resigned in 1988 in protest at what he termed as the "genocidal policies" of the International Monetary Fund in developing countries:

...food security has declined dramatically in all Third World regions, but in Africa in particular. Growing dependence on food imports, which is the lot of Sub-Saharan Africa, places these countries in an extremely vulnerable position. They simply do not have the foreign exchange to import enough food, given the fall in export prices and the need to repay debt. (thirdworldtraveler.com)

The colonial policy of production thus aggravated the shortage of industrialisation, which is an essential part of the process of development in this contemporary world of globalisation. Lack of industries created a dependency on imports of finished goods to meet the needs of the local population, which has been the case in most African countries. Indeed, during the colonial and immediate post-colonial period, the process of development in Sub-Saharan Africa was very weak, aggravated by the fact that the process of decolonisation left these countries very few known means and potential to embark on real development projects. This situation forced the majority of African countries to turn to their former colonisers and the West in general and their multinational companies for aid, in the form of loans that accumulate over time. Here lies the origin of Africa's excessive debt; yet over-indebtedness of a country is a major obstacle to its development.

Most African countries began to be indebted in the 1970s. The following table shows the debt crisis of the Third World.

Table 1: Towards the debt crisis - 1960 to 1980

	1960	1970	1980
Stock of external debt	8 billion $	70 billion $	540 billion $

Source: Committee for the Cancellation of Third World Debt (CADTM)[24]. (cadtm.org)

Africa's debt increased from independence between 1960 and 1980 for several reasons. The first is that Western governments and their international financial institutions applied a monetary policy of very low interest rates, which was very attractive to African countries and encouraged them to borrow more, as the revenue from their exports appeared to be increasing constantly, allowing them to repay the interest and capital, without much difficulty. However the revenue from African exports suddenly declined sharply because of falling prices on the world market, as shown in the table below.

Table 2: The fall in the prices of primary commodities exported by the South.

In constant dollars, 1985	Average annual change between 1977 and 2001	
Food	1.	2.6 %
Tropical drinks	2.	5.6 %
Cereal (grain) and oil	3.	3.5 %
Agricultural raw materials	4.	2.0 %
Metals, ores and minerals	5.	1.9 %

Source: Committee for the Cancellation of Third World Debt (cadtm.org)

---

[24] Comité pour l'Annulation de la Dette du Tiers Monde

When African countries began to borrow on financial markets in the 1970s, interest rates were between 3 and 4 percent; but in the late 1970s the economic and financial situation of the world suddenly changed. The second oil crisis which unfolded in the late 1970s and early 1980s further undermined the world economy, particularly that of Sub-Saharan Africa. It created imbalances in the macro-economic structures causing inflation, and increased trade and budget deficits. The crisis of that time was worsened by the recycling of the petrodollar;[25] and the United States took a unilateral decision in its fight against inflation, in order to overcome the economic crisis, but also, perhaps to reaffirm its leadership in the world especially in the economic domain after the failure of its foreign policies in Vietnam in 1975, and in Nicaragua and Iran in 1979. The governor of the United States' Federal Reserve, Mr Paul Volcker, announced a sharp increase in interest rates in the United States to attract capital and thus revive the economy. This policy provoked a sharp increase in the debt of African countries, because the interest rates on loans granted to them were variable and linked to U.S. interest rates. They jumped from 3 to 4 per cent in the 1970s to about 18 percent in the 1980s. Consequently, overnight Sub-Saharan Africa was forced to reimburse more than four times more interest. In the United Kingdom, Prime Minister Margaret Hilda Thatcher followed the United States policy, and the

---

[25]Unites States dollar earned from the sale of oil; it is simply oil revenues denominated in United States dollars. The term Petrodollars was coined in 1973 by Professor Ibrahim Oweiss of Georgetown University to describe the dollar earn by OPEC countries from the sale of oil.

monetary policy of the West became an entrapment for the African continent.

The reimbursement and servicing of the debt obtained in the 1970s, after these problems, became another issue. Most African countries could not meet their deadlines, and their debts quadrupled in the 1990s. Also the fact that they had to repay these debts in foreign currencies aggravated the problem because they used a large portion of the income derived from their exports, the prices of which, as we noted, were in continuous decline on international markets. Therefore Sub-Saharan African countries did not have sufficient income to repay their debts when deadlines arrived because of falling prices of commodities that would enable them to repay their debts. They were hence forced to request new loans in order to repay old ones, and thus had to turn to the IMF and the World Bank, the Paris Club, which constitutes Western governments, and the London Club, which brings together private banks of Western countries, in an unnatural partnership in their struggle to survive and reconstruct. The International Monetary Fund's intervention in Africa and other developing countries also became subject to strict conditions, especially in the mid-1980s, which increased the dependency of Africa on these institutions.

The 2004 report of the United Nations Conference on Trade and Development (UNCTAD) on African debt showed that the mechanism of debt impoverished the poor to enrich the rich:

Between 1970 and 2002, Africa received $ 540 billion of loans, but although it has paid nearly $550 billion in principal and interest, it still showed an outstanding debt of $ 295 billion in late 2002. The numbers are even more daunting for Sub-Saharan Africa, which having received $294 billion in loans and paid $268 billion in debt service, remains indebted to some $ 210 billion. (unctad.org).

As the debt increased significantly, the request for the intervention of the International Monetary Fund and the World Bank in Sub-Saharan Africa which became almost binding on Sub-Saharan Africans increased too. The operations of the International Monetary Fund took new directions because of the increase in interest rates on the international financial markets and the deteriorating terms of trade that translated themselves into the acceleration and generalisation of external budgetary and currency imbalances in most African countries.

We have noted that the initial objective of the founders of the International Bank for Reconstruction and Development, was to reconstruct European economies after the ruins of World War II; therefore, the promotion of socio-economic development of colonial Africa was initially not on The World Bank's agenda. The objectives of the Bank therefore evolved over the following years, due largely to the changes in the economic situation of post-war Europe and Japan. Consequently the Bank gradually focused on operations to combat poverty in developing countries. It "provides low cost loans to governments of middle-income and low-income countries that have a good credit rating." (worldbank.org)

The International Development Association (IDA), established in September 1960 (three years after the independence of the first Sub-Saharan African country, Ghana, in 1957 and three years before the founding of the Organisation of African Unity), is a component of the World Bank Group. Its primary objective is to promote development in developing countries, and it is complementary to the lending organ of the International Bank for Reconstruction and Development. It is:

> One of the largest sources of development finance, the IDA provides support for health, education, infrastructure, agriculture, economic, and institutional development to the world's poorest countries—half of which are in Africa. These countries are home to 2.5 billion people, 1.8 billion of whom survive on $2 a day or less. With the IDA's help, hundreds of millions of people have escaped poverty—through the creation of jobs, access to clean water, schools, roads, nutrition, electricity, and more. During the past decade, IDA funding immunized nearly half a billion children, provided access to better water sources for 123 million people, and helped 65 million people receive health services. (ibid)

The credits granted by the International Development Association do not bear interest, which should normally be beneficial to borrowers. It makes grants to developing countries to support the development of their economies and improve the living standards of their people. Its loans are also long-term with maturities of 20, 35 or even 40 years, with a period of 10 years as delay for the beginning of reimbursement, which should normally be very interesting for Africa.

The International Finance Corporation (IFC) which encourages private investment by offering different products to private companies in developing countries or countries in transition; the International Centre for Settlement of Investment Disputes (ICSID), responsible for resolving disputes between States and foreign investors; and the Multilateral Investment Guarantee Agency (MIGA), that provides (political) risk insurance guarantees for projects in a range of sectors in developing countries, are also institutions of the World Bank Group.

As for the International Monetary Fund (IMF), we have seen that its main role as an international multilateral institution is to help ensure international financial stability and to contribute to the promotion of economic growth, stability and the general level of employment in order to reduce poverty.

One of the first tasks of the International Monetary Fund is to provide financial assistance to countries that are in economic and/or financial crisis or difficulties. Therefore those countries that have problems with their balance of payments, or have serious economic problems in general can apply for loans and technical assistance from the International Monetary Fund to intervene in the management of their national economies.

We have noted here that the specific objectives of the two institutions at their inception were clearly defined and their missions were distinct. However, their operations, particularly in developing countries, had been more or less the same for more than thirty years, focusing on correcting balance of payment problems and on economic development as a common objective in their partnership and their operations in Sub-Saharan Africa.

Until 1980, the majority of International Monetary Fund operations were in the short term, while the World Bank had long term goals and its funding was unconditional without restrictive policies. The International Monetary Fund has been faithful to two objectives: the correction of payment imbalances, and the promotion and maintenance of prosperity. Its operations were basically financial, consisting temporarily in putting its resources at the disposal of member countries against sufficient guarantee to regulate imbalances in their balance of payments without compromising national prosperity or creating adverse effects at the international level. Another component of the Fund's operations focused on assisting "poor" countries in stabilising their economies and sustainably improving their standards of living. The creation of the Structural Adjustment Facility (SAF) and the Enhanced Structural Adjustment Facility (ESAF) has become an essential part of the Fund's work and led it to pay much attention to the plight of developing countries. Since the 1970s, the IMF has regulated balance of payment problems that many Member States were encountering by, according them, "concessional financing," which was provided by the Trust Fund from the mid-70s, then as of March 1986 they have been assured through the Structural Adjustment Facility (SAF) and then from 1987 by the Enhanced Structural Adjustment Facility (ESAF). The ESAF was replaced by the IMF's Poverty Reduction and Growth Facility

(PRGF)[26] in November 1999. "Altogether, 56 low-income countries benefited from the IMF's concessional assistance under the SAF and the ESAF, affecting nearly one billion people." (imf.org) Many African countries are part of the programme.

As we have noted, the operations of the World Bank, were in the long term, targeting economic growth through investment projects in basic sectors such as agriculture, education, energy, and infrastructure; it therefore financed investment rather than offering direct loans. The objectives of macro-economic adjustment policies of the World Bank were to strengthen the productive capacity of the economy and to increase its potential to directly promote supply, while those of the IMF were to maintain or stimulate demand to avoid deflation. However, if the management of anti-poverty programmes is now the responsibility of the World Bank and other development agencies, the International Monetary Fund also has a role to play in it, especially in the domain of macro-economic and financial policies. The two institutions "collaborate" with the governments of the countries concerned to implement programmes for "poverty reduction, economic growth, and debt relief." They collaborate to define the conditions for borrowing countries.

---

[26]The Poverty Reduction and Growth Facility (PRGF) is a loan of IMF to the world's poorest countries to, as the name indicates, reduce poverty in these countries. *To make its support more flexible and geared to the needs of Member States, the IMF replaced the PRGF with the Extended Credit Facility (ECF), that provides financial assistance to countries with protracted balance of payments problems. The ECF will be in line with the objectives of a country's own poverty reduction strategy.*

The World Bank and the International Monetary Fund are over sixty years old now. Like most post-war inter-governmental institutions, they are not immune to criticism vis-à-vis their relations with the South, especially Sub-Saharan Africa. The two institutions have been accused of having a negative impact on developing countries.

Milton Friedman[27] and Joseph E. Stiglitz[28] both criticised the functioning of the International Monetary Fund and the World Bank. Joseph Stiglitz preferred to resign rather than endorse policies that do not emanate from democratic debate in the countries concerned, and that involve economists putting themselves above scientific debate. (sandovalhernandezj.people.cofc.edu) Other critics argue that without the International Monetary Fund, there might have been isolated cases of economic problems in the South, but not a crisis of such a magnitude. The general idea was that the programmes of reform of the International Monetary Fund and the World Bank are based more on political considerations than economic ones, and that these programmes exacerbate crises in developing countries. Their credibility was thus questioned by a majority of observers, including some of their own employees[29] which almost tarnished their images.

---

[27]Milton Friedman (July 31, 1912 – November 16, 2006) was an American economist statistician and writer. He taught at the University of Chicago for more than three decades. He won the Nobel Memorial Prize in Economics in 1976. He is well known for his research on consumption analysis, monetary history and theory, and the complexity of stabilisation policy.

[28]American economist, Nobel Laureate (2001), Vice-President and Chief Economist of the World Bank from 1997 to 2000.

[29]Joseph E. Stiglitz and Davison Budhoo were staff of the IMF and the World Bank respectively. Budhoo resigned in 1988 in protest against he called the "genocidal policies" of the IMF in poor countries.

In preparation for the Golden Jubilee of the World Bank, eleven African Heads of State met in Libreville, Gabon, on 27 May 1993, with the American Civil Rights activist, Mr. Jesse Jackson. During this meeting, Jesse Jackson ironically denounced the effects of the policies of the World Bank and the International Monetary Fund on developing countries, especially in Africa. According to him: "They used to use the bullet or the rope ... now they use the World Bank and the International Monetary Fund." (socialistalternative.org) Both institutions have been accused of being under the influence of the United States and the European Union to advance their economic and political interests. The late Mr Jesse Helms, former Chairman of the Foreign Affairs Committee of the United States Senate, said before the Security Council of the United Nations in January 2000 that, the organisation is an instrument of the foreign policy of the United States. (derechos.org)

Isabelle Grunberg,[30] for her part, argued that:

Executive directors (representatives of States) at IMF readily admit that their lending decisions closely follow the recommendations of Washington. The grant (or the threat of refusal) of these loans are typically used to strengthen military alliances in the United States or to obtain concessions, especially commercial. Thus, and to open foreign markets, the United States can provide to offer reciprocal concessions in the framework of the World Trade Organization (WTO).[31] (monde-diplomatique.fr)

---

[30] Isabelle Grunberg is a senior policy adviser in the Office of Development Studies at the United Nations Development Programme. She was formerly Associate Director of United Nations studies at Yale University and a MacArthur fellow and lecturer at Yale.

[31] Les directeurs exécutifs (représentants des États) au FMI reconnaissent

She continues to accuse the IMF of conducting an economic policy of "veritable redistribution in favour of the rich, both at the national and global levels. At the national level, this inappropriate and unfavourable redistribution is a direct consequence of the economic programmes that are the invariable core of the conditions imposed." (ibid)

Davison Budhoo summarised the effects of the International Monetary Fund and the World Bank operations on developing countries while confirming Isabelle Grunberg's propositions:

> Instead of development and favourable adjustment, the Third World today is in an accelerated spiral of economic and social decline. That decline is linked directly to the World Bank and the International Monetary Fund. IMF-World Bank structural adjustment programs (SAPs) are designed to reduce consumption in developing countries and to redirect resources to manufacturing exports for the repayment of debt. This has caused overproduction of primary products and a precipitous fall in their prices. It has also led to the devastation of traditional agriculture and to the emergence of hordes of landless farmers in virtually every country in which the World Bank and IMF operate. (thirdworldtraveler.com)

Here Budhoo shows that the production policy, as we can observe, is not very different from the one

volontiers que leurs décisions de prêts suivent étroitement les recommandations de Washington. L'octroi (ou la menace du refus) de ces prêts sont classiquement utilisés pour renforcer les alliances militaires des États-Unis ou pour obtenir des concessions, notamment commerciales. Ainsi, et pour ouvrir les marchés extérieurs, les États-Unis peuvent se dispenser d'offrir des concessions réciproques dans le cadre de l'Organisation mondiale du commerce (OMC).

established by the colonialists. During Colonisation, the metropolis encouraged a culture for export neglecting and discouraging crops for local consumption. This new version promoted by the Structural Adjustment Programme of the International Monetary Fund and the World Bank is geared towards the reduction of local consumption, instead of directly discouraging the growth of crops for local consumption. The purpose of this policy is therefore not very different from that of its predecessor since both are intended to "redistribute resources towards manufacturing industries for export." The colonial policy created a shortage of crops for local consumption, while the new programme reduces their consumption, therefore, generating over-production and the inevitable effect according to the laws of demand and supply was falling prices of the products, which has seriously affected the reimbursement of the debt, and hence aggravated the indebtedness of Sub-Saharan Africa.

The Structural Adjustment Programme (SAP)

It would be utterly unfair to say, without reservation, despite these criticisms, that the IMF and the World Bank have brought nothing positive to the African continent. When they started their operations in Africa in the late 1970s, their main purpose was, according to the Berg report of the World Bank published in 1981, to promote development. The purposes of the two institutions suggested at the onset of their interventions in Africa that they had come to help the continent solve its economic and financial problems: balance of payment difficulties, debt crisis of the 1970s, poverty, chronic unemployment, caused by several factors notably the fluctuations in commodity prices and rising interest rates. Their activities should therefore normally be beneficial to Africa.

To assess the effects of the International Monetary Fund and the World Bank on the process of African reconstruction, we should take into account the Structural Adjustment Programme (SAP) which is the basis of their interventions. The SAP is a programme of economic reform according to the context to allow countries facing economic crises to find a solution to their problems. Its provisions act either on the conjuncture or on the structures of the economies and are based on "negotiation" between the Fund and the Bank, on the one hand, and the countries concerned, on the other, to solve their economic problems. The credits granted in the programme are called Structural or Sectoral Adjustment Loans (SAL), and are released in instalments in accordance with the agreement. Since the Structural Adjustment Programme is a contract based on negotiations, it is supposed to be an agreement formulated by the parties involved in the form of partnership, and then submitted to the Board of Governors in a "letter of intent" stipulating the commitment of the country concerned in complying with the conditions. It is therefore a programme of economic transformation for the countries concerned.

To better understand the nature of the basic interventions of the International Monetary Fund, for example, especially in Africa vis-à-vis its Structural Adjustment Programme, we will get into the context of international trade in its simple form. According to the classical theory of international trade, when exports and imports equalise, the balance of payments is said to be in equilibrium. For an international exchange agreement between countries, companies or even individuals of different nationalities, a currency in which the transaction will be done is chosen. For example, in the case of transactions between The Gambia and the United Kingdom, it may be the Pound Sterling, the Dollar or the Dalasi or even the Euro. For these transactions, the banks of The Gambia should have the Pound in stock, and British banks should under normal circumstances also hold reserves of the Dalasi, which is the currency of The Gambia to be able to purchase goods and services in The Gambia. If The Gambia sells goods or a service abroad, it will normally receive the local currency (Dalasi) in exchange. The rates at which The Gambian and British banks exchange the Dalasi and the Pound Sterling are determined on the Stock Exchange and on an interbank market.[32] Depending on

---

[32] The financial system dealing with the trading of currencies among banks and

the laws of demand and supply, the more the products or services of a country are demanded, the more its currency gains value, consequently causing a rise in the price of this currency. It is very unlikely that the amount of The Gambia's imports from the United Kingdom or other countries will be equal to its exports to that country or other countries. If The Gambia exports more than it imports, its trade balance will be positive; but if it imports more than it exports, the trade balance will be negative. This means that the stock of the Pound Sterling at the Central Bank of The Gambia will reduce. If it is zero, The Gambia no longer has the means to pay for imports and will be in default of payment. However, credit in foreign currency granted to the Central Bank of The Gambia can remedy the situation. Obviously, the Central Bank of The Gambia will, in this situation, try to buy the Pound by selling its currency. If the Pound is increasingly demanded, then more Dalasi will be required to buy one Pound. And the Pound will increase in value and price. The consequence is that the import price will be high, and British goods will become more expensive for The Gambia. To remedy this situation, The Gambia will import fewer goods from the UK to buy fewer pounds. However, if the imports required are products or services of first necessity, such as medicine, staple food, raw materials for a strategic industry, this is one of the cases in which The Gambia will request the intervention of the International Monetary Fund to help remedy the situation. To receive

---

other financial institutions; this does not include retail investors and other small traders. Some interbank trading is carried out by banks on behalf of large customers, but most interbank trading takes place from the accounts of the banks.

assistance from the IMF, The Gambia must necessarily abide by the conditions of the Structural Adjustment Programme, which are recommendations based on the "Washington Consensus,"[33] for reforms and restructuring.

According to the International Monetary Fund and the World Bank, these reforms and restructuring are necessary, and guide the countries concerned to apply fiscal and monetary discipline to avoid engagements that would aggravate their economic problems. The principal idea is to guide the countries with budget deficits, capital gains or currency depreciation, not to engage in activities that are likely to worsen their balance of payment problems. The Structural Adjustment Programme that, as we have just seen, is deemed necessary to not waste the efforts of the International Monetary Fund, mostly obliges the borrowing country to adhere to the requirements of the Washington Consensus. They are: creation of a stable and competitive exchange rate; trade liberalisation; liberalisation of financial markets; privatisation; fiscal discipline; orientation of public expenditure for economic growth and the equitable distribution of revenues; tax reforms in order to obtain a broad tax base and low tax rate; removal of barriers to trade and investment at international level; deregulation, and protection of private property.

---

[33]The American economist John Williamson, in 1989 proposed ten recommendations to countries whose economies are in difficulty, especially Latin American countries, known as the Washington Consensus. According to Williamson these recommendations represent the opinion of most experts from international financial institutions such as the World Bank and the International Monetary Fund, as well as financial institutions in the USA.

This Structural Adjustment Programme (SAP) that visibly forces borrowing countries to reduce social services and programmes to the bare minimum, transforms health and education to paid services, gets rid of subsidies on food, implements fiscal austerity, privatises certain sectors of their public companies considered ineffective, opens their markets to goods, services and capital, surely generated effects. However, is the SAP solely responsible for the economic problems and poverty in Africa? What are the consequences of these conditions for Sub-Saharan Africa today submerged by its debts?

From an economic perspective, devaluation is often accompanied by an increase in prices of goods and services in the local economy, especially imported goods and services, which put them out of reach of the majority of the population. Liberalisation of businesses means the dismantling of tariffs and other regulations; which, without compensation, is often at the expense of less developed partners. Therefore, protectionism is sometimes necessary, especially for industries that are not strong enough to compete with foreign companies, as Joseph Stiglitz indicated in his work entitled *Globalization and its Discontents*:

> ...most of the advanced industrial countries – including the United States and Japan - had built up their economies by wisely and selectively protecting some of their industries until they were strong enough to compete with foreign companies. While blanket protectionism has often not worked for countries that have tried it, neither has rapid trade liberalisation. Forcing a developing country to open itself up to imported products that would compete with those

produced by certain of its industries, industries that were dangerously vulnerable to competition from much stronger counterpart industries in other countries, can have disastrous consequences – socially and economically. Jobs have systematically been destroyed – poor farmers in developing countries simply couldn't compete with the highly subsidized goods from Europe and America – before the countries' industrial and agricultural sectors were able to grow strong and create new jobs. (16, 17)

Privatisation, especially of public enterprises and assets, symbolises the arrival of foreign companies that are mostly interested more in profit than social welfare. If privatisation and the reduction of public sector activities are carried out without adequate regulation, which is usually the case with the Structural Adjustment Programme in Africa, they inevitably lead to reforms of the labour market, creation of job insecurity and layoffs, generally weakening the position of workers, and reducing real wages and resulting in precariousness. The goods and services produced by the foreign companies that take over generally become relatively more expensive for the majority of the population, because these new companies do not possess the social vocation aspect of public companies, especially in the context of private monopolies, which occurs in the absence of competition. The privatisation of public enterprises can, even if it temporarily brings money to the public treasury, therefore represent a loss in a social context. In addition, it limits the capacity and ability of the State to intervene in its own economy to stabilise it. Opening African markets to foreign investment often puts the major part of the public heritage of these countries within the reach of foreigners, especially when this is done as it is often, without control or norms. Joseph Stiglitz argues that:

> The Western countries have pushed poor countries to eliminate trade barriers, but kept up their own barriers, preventing developing countries from exporting their agricultural products and so depriving them of desperately needed export income. The United States was, of course, one of the prime culprits, and this was an issue about which I felt intensely. When I was chairman of the Council of Economic Advisers, I fought hard against this hypocrisy. It not only hurt the developing countries; it also cost America... (6)

The lack of assistance from the government in an atmosphere of precarious liberalisation greatly affects local industries, especially small and medium-sized businesses that provide the bulk of national employment. Not having the power and support to compete with imports that are often subsidised, especially when they come from the West, nor having access to investment in the form of credit, national businesses fall into bankruptcy. Also, when interest rates are not backed by effective monetary policy, they rise and push small and medium-sized local companies into bankruptcy, causing an increase in unemployment. It is equally obvious that deregulation reduces or eliminates the guarantees for employment.

Unlike ordinary loans, the Structural Adjustment Facility (SAF), and the Enhanced Structural Adjustment Facility (ESAF)[34] are economic policies and

---

[34]An arrangement through which the International Monetary Fund

programmes, and have growth objectives rather than quantitative ones. However, the definition of the means and the economic programmes employed to achieve their objectives, always interfere with the domestic affairs of the borrowing countries. For example, to achieve the growth objectives, the programme of economic policy is defined for a period of at least three years. Yet we have seen that these objectives are in the framework of the Structural Adjustment Programme as institutional preconditions for the continuous interventions of the Bank and especially the IMF, most often in the logic of the Washington Consensus. They provide loans to countries in difficulty based on purely economic considerations. In fact, the IMF and the World Bank operate according to economic liberalism, whose fundamental principle is that there is a natural order which drives the economic system toward equilibrium. For example, the law of demand and supply leads production and consumption to equilibrium in an atmosphere of free trade and competition that guarantees the optimum adjustment of available resources (supply) to demand. According to this liberal principle, then the market is able to provide the necessary equilibrium for economic development.

Even if the SAF and ESAF are effective instruments in technically assisting poor countries surmount financial and economic difficulties, the power of the

---

(IMF)provides medium-term concessional loans (5 to 10 years) for poorer countries to adjust their balance of payments. It was introduced in 1987, and follows the same principle as the Structural Adjustment Facility (SAF) which was introduced in 1986, but it has tripled the resources and monitors the performance of borrowers more closely. About 65 countries are eligible for assistance under the ESAF.

IMF and the Bank remains indisputable, because, as we have pointed out, the remaining tranches of the credit are granted only when the borrowing countries respect the conditions. The IMF and the World Bank, in turn, impose conditions for the countries concerned to maintain a balanced budget and solve other economic problems.

Also, sometimes the Bretton Woods institutions pay no or little attention to the political and socio-cultural situations of the countries receiving their assistance. The World Bank sometimes provides funds to military regimes and governments that openly violate the principles of human rights and carry out socio-economic policies that hamper development in Africa. In 1966, it ignored resolutions of the Assembly General of the United Nations, and granted loans to countries engaged in a flagrant violation of the UN Charter. The white (minority) segregationist regime in South Africa engaged in war against the black (majority) South African nationalists that were fighting against the apartheid regime, yet the World Bank granted a loan of $20 million to the South African apartheid regime. Another loan of $10 million was granted to Portugal carrying out a war in Angola and Mozambique against the anti-colonialists. Even if the Bank justified its action in accordance with Section 10 of Article IV of the IBRD Articles of Agreement, which allowed neither intervention "in the political affairs of any Member State, nor to be influenced in their decisions by political orientation," these activities were not productive, neither from a logical nor a socio-economic point of view.

Also the paradox is that the Washington Consensus, which is the basis of the Structural Adjustment Programme, was initiated by a group of government officials and economists of the United States, the World Bank and the International Monetary Fund, who, even if they are professional economists, knew very little about the economies of developing countries. Most of the personalities who pioneered the Washington Consensus, Robert Edward Rubin, Roger C. Altman and Nicholas Brady, are from Wall Street[35] and work for investment companies. Ernest Stern was a former senior official of the World Bank who worked for the bank for 23 years and then became director of the J.P. Morgan Bank. Sir James David Wolfensohn was the 9th president of the World Bank between May 1995 and June 2005, and had managed J. Henry Schroder & Co. in New York, another investment bank. Yet these economists had no consultation with economists from the countries concerned by the SAP. Moreover, as Joseph Stiglitz has indicated:

> The choice of heads for these institutions symbolises the institutions' problem, and too often has contributed to their dysfunction. While almost all of the activities of IMF and the World Bank today are in the developing world (certainly, all of their lending), they are led by representatives from the industrialised nations [...]They are chosen behind closed doors, and

---

[35] Wall Street is a street in lower Manhattan; it is the financial district of New York that is the original home of the New York Stock Exchange. It is named after the wooden wall Dutch colonists built in this area in 1653 to defend themselves from the British and Native Americans. Being the historic headquarters of the largest U.S. brokerages and investment banks, and many having since relocated to other areas of Manhattan, over time, Wall Street has become a metonym for the financial markets of the United States as a whole.

it has never been viewed as a prerequisite that the head should have any experience in the developing world. The institutions are not representative of the nations they serve. (19)

The Washington Consensus has never been ratified, not even debated by the governments of the countries on which it is imposed. Many critics therefore see it as a strategic idea that the West imposed on the South regardless to the situation and economic and social conditions of the countries affected, as this African diplomat put it:

You can't take something, an idea from one country and transplant it in another country. It doesn't work; you have to do a study to see what are the good things and the bad things about this particular idea. We are completely different people. It does not mean that because this model succeeded in America or in Europe that it would succeed in Africa. We have completely different ideas about doing things, it's the same as with democracy. Yet if you look at China, they are not listening to these people, but they are booming economically, and they have their own communist agenda. They have the control over their economy. Who says that it's only when you have democracy that you ensure socio-economic development? (Personal interview, 20 June 2007.)

We have emphasised that the Structural Adjustment Programme of the IMF and the Bank has been based on the liberal concept of economics. Free trade in the context of normal globalisation is considered a stimulus for economic growth that usually benefits the population. However, the social effects resulting from the implementation of the Structural Adjustment Programme have usually been negative, especially because liberalisation has been done in an indiscriminate manner. Even if growth follows, a large part of the population do not usually benefit from it. And if by the way, for example, the programme advocated by the Fund bears its fruit on the volume of exports and the balance of payments, there is no evidence that the population would actually benefit from the growth in many African countries, without some aspect of social democracy and the equitable redistribution of resources.

The structure and functioning of the International Monetary Fund and the World Bank

We have seen that the IMF and the World Bank, like most organisations, are composed of several organs, namely the Board of Governors, the Board of Directors, Ministerial Committees, Directors and the Independent Evaluation Office (IEO) of the IMF.

The Boards of Governors of the IMF and the World Bank consist of one governor and one alternate governor for each Member State; they are the supreme governing bodies of the institutions. The governors are often the Ministers of Finance or governors of the Central Banks of the Member States. The Boards of Governors of the two institutions usually meet once a year, to review the work of their respective institutions. The annual meetings, which take place in September or October, are usually held in Washington for two consecutive years and then in another Member State every three years. (imf.org) The Board of Governors often delegates its powers to the Board of Directors, but maintains the right to approve amendments to the Statute and the general regulations of the institutions, increases in quotas, the admission of new members, the obligatory retirement of members and allocations of Special Drawing Rights (SDRs).[36] They play the role of

---

[36]The SDR is an international reserve asset of the IMF, created in 1969 by the IMF to support the Bretton Woods fixed exchange rate system and to supplement Member States' official reserves. Its value is based on a basket of four key international currencies, and SDRs can be exchanged for freely usable currencies. With a general SDR allocation that took effect on August 28 "and a special allocation on September 9, 2009, the amount of SDRs increased from SDR 21.4 billion to around SDR 204 billion (equivalent to about $309 billion, converted using the rate of September 10, 2013.")

supreme referee in matters concerning the interpretation of the Articles of Agreement of the IMF and the Bank.

The Board of Executive Directors (the Board) of the IMF is responsible for conducting the day-to-day running of the institution. It comprises 24 directors, appointed or elected by Member States or by groups of countries, with the Managing Director serving as its Chairman. The Board holds several meetings each week and does its work largely on the basis of documents prepared by IMF management and staff. The Board of the World Bank is made up of 25 Executive Directors, representing Member States of the World Bank. They are responsible for overseeing the overall orientation of the institutions on a day-to-day basis, as well as the application of the policy defined by the Member States through the Boards of Governors. They approve all policies and strategies, lending operations, as well as its institutional budgets and audits. They also deal with discussions on operation evaluations, development trends, and strategic directions for the Bank.

The Boards make their decisions by consensus in a normal situation, and they organise formal votes, publishing a "Summary of the President," which is a summary of the views of the Boards. Informal discussions are sometimes held as preliminary discussions of complex issues. The Executive Directors also formally appoint the President of the World Bank, who serves as Chair of the Boards of Directors, even though the United States Government actually selects and nominates the candidate. The Executive Directors are representatives of the Member States of the institutions that appointed or elected them, and hence they represent the interests of those countries, as well as the general interest of the Fund and the Bank, which render them a double role. They are responsible for the running of the general operations of the Bank and exercise all the powers delegated to them by the Board of Governors.

The third organ is the Ministerial Committee whose role is to advise the Board of Governors. It has two branches: the International Monetary and Financial Committee (IMFC) and the Development Committee (DC). The IMFC consists of 24 members from the group of governors representing all the 188 Member States. Member States are represented in the same manner as in the Board of Directors. The Committee meets twice a year to review the state of the global economy; it advises the IMF about the orientation of its work. At the end of each meeting the IMFC publishes a statement on its views, defining the orientation of its programme for the next six months. It functions through consensus, and does not conduct any formal vote.

Table 01: Composition of the International Monetary and Financial Committee of the IMF (IMFC).

Singapore(Chair)	Canada	Italy	South Africa
Algeria	China	Japan	Spain
Argentina	France	Korea	Sweden
Austria	Gabon	Malaysia	Switzerland
Belgium	Germany	Russia	United Arab Emirates

Brazil	India	Saudi Arabia	United Kingdom
			United States

Source: (imf.org)

Amongst the members of the IMFC we can see that there are three countries from Africa i.e. 2 from Sub-Saharan Africa (South Africa and Gabon) and one country from North Africa (Algeria).

The Development Committee is a forum of the World Bank Group and the International Monetary Fund at ministerial level for inter-governmental consensus building on issues of development. It is known formally as the Joint Ministerial Committee of the Boards of Governors of the World Bank and the International Monetary Fund on the transfer of resources. It was established in 1974, with a mandate to advise the Boards of Governors of the Bank and the Fund on development issues and on the resources required to promote development in emerging and developing countries. Over the years, the Committee has included trade and environmental issues.

Table 02: Composition of the Development Committee (CD)

Poland (Chair)	Ivory Coast	Malaysia	Saudi Arabia
Bahrain	Finland	Morocco	Spain
Belgium	France	Netherlands	Switzerland
Bolivia	Germany	New Zealand	United Kingdom

Brazil	India	Nigeria	United States
Canada	Italy	Russia	Zambia
China	Japan		

Source: (imf.org)

The Development Committee contains four African members, three from Sub-Saharan Africa (Ivory Coast, Nigeria and Zambia) and one Member State from North Africa (Morocco).

The IMF's Managing Director serves both as chairman of the Executive Board and Head of Staff. He or she is assisted by four Deputy Managing Directors, responsible for the daily running of the Fund. The IMF's Governors and Executive Directors may nominate nationals of any Member State of the Fund; and the Board of Executive Directors may select a Managing Director by a majority of votes cast, but in the past the Board has made appointments by consensus. As for the World Bank Group, it has a President, assisted by two Vice Presidents: Vice President Institutional Integrity and Vice President & Auditor-General, Internal Audit, who manage the institution. The Managing Director of the IMF and the President of the World Bank Group are appointed by the Board of (Executive) Directors for a renewable term of five years.

The Independent Evaluation Office (IEO) was created in 2001 to conduct independent and objective assessments of the activities and policies of the International Monetary Fund. It is entirely independent from IMF management and has no direct link of dependence to the Board of Executive Directors. Its mission is to build a culture of learning, enhance the external credibility of the IMF, promote a better understanding of its actions, and encourage corporate governance and supervision of the IMF.

The IMF and World Bank make decisions according to a census or weight voting system, in that Member States possess voting weights in relation to their financial contributions ("share"), which are based broadly on their relative sizes in the world economy, and determines their contribution to the financial resources of the institutions. The voting weight of a Member State in decision-making is proportional to its financial contributions, i.e. its share or quota. Thus, the United States, quasi main contributor to the IMF, possesses nearly 20 percent of the voting rights before the reform of the IMF's voting system. It is worth noting that out of the 188 Member States, the ten largest contributors possess the majority of the voting rights to themselves alone.

While most of the decisions of the two institutions are made unanimously in consultation with each other, the modalities imply a majority consisting of 85 percent of voting rights. This voting system relating to the financial share or contribution of a Member State clearly shows that the IMF and the World Bank are far from being fully democratic institutions. The fact that their decision-making and functioning have been based on the financial contributions of their Member States hinders Africa's capacity to exercise power or play its rightful role in them.

The reform of the IMF voting system, which had been claimed by Africa and other parties in the same situation, actually began in 2006, when the Member States adhered to the idea of redistributing quotas and hence voting power within the institution. In 2008, the reform of quotas and representation foresaw "a limited increase of quotas of a group of emerging countries as well as measures to increase the representation of low-income countries," which took effect in March 2011. (imf.org) In accordance with this reform, some countries had their voting rights increased after the United States accepted voting rights of 17 percent.[37] This reform sought to strengthen the credibility of the IMF decision-making process, but it was not advantageous to the African continent. None of the African Member States, not even Nigeria or South Africa, were among the top ten. The only country that is included in the general list is South Africa with a share of less than 1 percent (0.87). In fact, with this new system that increased the voting rights allocated to some members regardless to their national wealth, Africa remains as marginalised in the IMF-World Bank systems as before.

Going along, it is interesting to note the composition of the Boards of Directors of both institutions responsible for overseeing their orientation on a daily basis and for their budgets, and lending policies. They comprise representatives of the five largest shareholders

[37]After this reform the countries that have the most voting rights are as follows: The United States 17.08% Japan 6.13% Germany 5.99% France 4.95%; Britain 4.95%, Italy 3.25%, Canada 2.94%, Russia 2.74%, the Netherlands 2.38%, Belgium 2.13%, India 1.92%; Brazil, 1.41% South Africa 0.87%. Countries whose voting rights are increasing are China, 2.94% to 3.65%, Mexico 1.20% to 1.43%, South Korea 0.76% to 1.33% and Turkey 0.45% to 0.55%.

(the United States, Germany, France, Japan, and the United Kingdom) as permanent members. The People's Republic of China, the Russian Federation, and Saudi Arabia as "single constituency" Board chairs also have their own permanent seats, and another 16 directors are elected for a two-year term. The whole of Sub-Saharan Africa is represented by just three Executive Directors.

The International Monetary Fund and the World Bank are also not as transparent as we might have imagined, because most of their documents are for internal use. When a country needs funding from these institutions, it is their officials who are said to define the programmes that will accompany the funding, in collaboration with the governments concerned. Nonetheless, projects are elaborated technically, before being submitted to vote by the Board of Directors. This shows that neither the national representatives of the borrowing countries, nor their civil institutions are involved in the elaboration of the structural adjustment plans that they must adhere to. When the votes on the programme are carried out, the documents have already been prepared and members of the Board must accept or reject them. Depending on the legal status of IMF loans, documents drawn between the IMF and Member States are not international agreements. Borrowing countries therefore have no legal obligation to commit to them. The problem, however, is that the IMF and the World Bank are often the only lenders of that kind to be solicited by Member States in need, especially those in Sub-Saharan Africa, a position that attributes them a status of monopoly. This feature shows that the influence or control of these institutions of the Bretton Woods system on borrowing countries is enormous.

The documents on the adjustment plans are not directly debated, not even discussed in national parliaments, which means that the actions of the IMF and the World Bank do not require any form of ratification by national governments. The responsibility of the IMF or the Bank vis-à-vis these programmes depends neither on national parliaments of borrowing countries, nor on their citizens, but on their main shareholders, which are mostly Western governments and their international financial institutions.

The critics of the census voting system have a point. The decisions of the IMF and the Bank are made by vote of the Board of Governors or the Board of Executive Directors representing Member States, and the weight of the vote of a Member State is proportional to its share or voting weight. The fact that important decisions require a majority of 70 to 85 percent, and the United States having alone 17 per cent of the vote, out of the Member States possessing the majority of the votes after the reform indicates therefore that it still has de facto, veto power. Countries in the eurozone have less influence because of, perhaps, lack of coordination amongst them, yet they collectively account for 22.66 percent of the shares, which should have given them significant weight in the IMF decision-making process, had they put their voices together. Theoretically, therefore, the IMF is under the control of the United States and other Western countries. The votes of Member States being proportional to their contributions to the resources of the institutions clearly indicates that its decisions are controlled or at least influenced by these countries that make the major contribution. This is based on the "He who pays the piper calls the tune" doctrine, in that if you pay for someone's services, you can dictate exactly what you want that person to do, which is completely out of the context of democracy and reasonable social principles. This is especially crucial for the other members, notably Africans, whose contributions are smaller, but require the assistance of the IMF almost on a permanent basis.

In a normal decision-making process in a nation, the democratic electoral system does not distinguish between rich and poor; every citizen has one vote equal to that of any other, rich or poor, and yet everyone proportionately pays their taxes in most societies according to their resources and wealth, wealthier citizens paying more taxes and the less wealthy paying less. In the IMF and the World Bank systems, it is quite the opposite. Their voting system is based on no notion of social democracy, because countries that contribute more money to their maintenance have more say in their decision-making process, which is not even based on the principles of positive economics, but on those of capitalism and political strategy.

At the World Bank and IMF, there is a rule, which is very real, even if it is not written. As indicated in the following tables, the president of the World Bank Group is always an American, while the Director of the IMF is always European.

Table 03: Presidents of the World Bank since its inception.

N°	Name	Nationality	Term
01	Eugene Meyer	USA	June 1946 – Dec. 1946
02	John J. McCloy	USA	1947 – 1949
03	Eugene R. Black	USA	1949 – 1963

04	George D. Woods	USA	1963 – 1968
05	Robert S. McNamara	USA	1968 – 1981
06	Alden W. Clausen	USA	1981 – 1986
07	Barber B. Conable	USA	1986 – 1991
08	Lewis T. Preston	USA	1991 – 1995
09	James Wolfensohn	USA	1995 – 2005
10	Paul Wolfowitz	USA	2005 – 2007
11	Robert Zoellick	USA	2007 – 2012
12	Jim Young Kim*	USA	2012 to present

* U.S. citizen, born abroad.

Among the 12 presidents of the World Bank, appointed since its inception, only the 9th, James Wolfensohn and the current President Jim Young Kim, were not born on United States soil; they are American by naturalisation. James Wolfensohn was born in Sydney, Australia, on December 1, 1933, and Jim Young Kim was born in Seoul, South Korea on December 8, 1959.

Member States of the World Bank expressed their commitment in 2011 to choosing a president in an "open, transparent and merit-based" process.[38] (liberation.fr) Former Nigerian Finance Minister Ngozi Okonjo-Iweala, a renowned economist who had spent two terms as Finance Minister of Nigeria, and 25 years

---

[38] «...ouverte, transparente et fondée sur le mérite».

of her career at the Bank and has served as Director General from 2007 to 2011, attempted to lift the taboo by contesting the position of President of the World Bank Group. It would have been a remarkably positive contribution to African reparation, if Ngozi Okonjo-Iweala had been appointed President of the World Bank Group. But even before the election, she admitted that the choice of President "is not really based on merit, but on political weight and for that reason, the United States will win it." (ibid) Indeed the US president, Barack Obama, selected Jim Young Kim for the presidency of the World Bank Group.

Table 04: Director General of the IMF since its inception

N°	Name	Nationality	Term
01	Camille Gutt	Belgian	1946 – 1951
02	Ivar Rooth	Swedish	1951 – 1956
03	Per Jacobsson	Swedish	1956 – 1963
04	Pierre-Paul Schweitzer	French	1963 – 1973
05	H. Johannes Witteveen	Dutch	1973 – 1978
06	Jacques de Larosière	French	1978 –1987
07	Michel Camdessus	French	1987 – 2000
08	Stanley Fischer	USA (interim)	14/02–30/04/ 2000
09	Horst Köhler	German	2000 – 2004
10	Anne Krueger,	USA (interim)	04/03–07/06/ 2004
11	Rodrigo Rato,	Spanish	2004 – 2007
12	Dominique Strauss-Kahn	French	2007 – 2011
13	John Lipsky	USA (interim)	15/05/–

			05/07/2011
14	Christine Lagarde	French	2011 to present

Equally, since the creation of the International Monetary Fund, the post of Director General has always been occupied by a European, with only three American interim directors, which is normal, because when problems occur at the management of the IMF, the interim is assured by the Assistant Director, a post always held by an American. The Director of the IMF is traditionally European, against all logic of democracy as well as the provision of the decision-making process, that stipulates that the governors and directors of the IMF can "nominate nationals of any member country of the institution" (imf.org). Industrialised countries still monopolise power within it, since the representatives of the ten most powerful countries (contributors) carry more than 60 percent of the voting rights on the Board of Directors.

During the fourth summit of the forum of Brazil, Russia, India, China and South Africa, (BRICS) held in March 2012, in New Delhi, the declaration of Heads of State and Government of the so-called emerging economies:

...criticises the 'slowness of reforms at the International Monetary Fund' (IMF) expected to further open up the institution to the South. While the campaign was launched to replace the American, Robert Zoellick, in June, at the head of the World Bank, the BRICS demand a selection process that is 'open' and 'based on merit', an implicit criticism of the tradition under which Americans and Europeans share, up to now, the management of the World Bank and the IMF. (lemonde.fr)[39]

Moreover, as we have seen, the United States almost has a veto power and can thus block almost all decisions. The fact that there is little or no source of funding outside the IMF and the World Bank for countries in difficulty, gives these institutions almost absolute influence on the governments of the countries in need. The IMF is a lender of last resort, meaning that when a country requests its intervention, that country's balance of payments is in difficulty, its currency is under pressure and its debt discourages investors, hence the active clients of the IMF are in economic danger. Under such conditions, they have the power to oblige their clients to comply with SAP, even if that hampers the process of development in the country concerned.

The Marshall Plan[40] was largely responsible for the success of the reconstruction of Western Europe after World War II, with very little intervention of the World Bank and the International Monetary Fund. In fact, the IMF and the Bank have been trying to realise in Sub-

---

[39] ...critique ainsi la *'lenteur des réformes du Fonds monétaire international'* (FMI) censées ouvrir davantage l'institution sur le Sud. Alors que la campagne est lancée pour remplacer l'Américain Robert Zoellick, en juin, à la tête de la Banque mondiale, les BRICS réclament un processus de sélection *'ouvert'* et *'basé sur le mérite'*, critique implicite de la tradition en vertu de laquelle Américains et Européens se partagent jusqu'à présent les directions de la Banque mondiale et du FMI.

[40] The Marshall Plan (officially known as the European Recovery Programme, ERP) was the initiative of the United States, named after Secretary of State George Marshall, to aid Europe by giving economic support to help rebuild war-devastated regions in Europe after World War II, remove trade barriers, modernise industry, and make Europe's devastated economies prosperous again, in order to prevent the spread of Soviet influence and Communism. The plan began in 1948 and ran for four years.

Saharan Africa what the Marshall Plan had done in Europe. However unlike the strategies of the Marshall Plan, the Structural Adjustment Programme of the IMF requires borrowing countries to liberalise their commercial sectors and accept the free conversion of their currencies without adequate control. In some countries affected massively by World War II, like Germany and Japan, the governments introduced free trade at the time of the Marshall Plan. The German Minister of Economy, Mr Ludwig Erhard, for example, implemented essentially what the IMF is imposing on most of Africa today. Germany eliminated price controls, stabilised its currency, reduced income tax and introduced free trade; Japan did the same. What we can infer from this is that the economic programmes of the post-war era, in those countries severely affected by the war, indicated that free trade rapidly generated economic growth. This implies that the Structural Adjustment Programme should be implemented in an atmosphere of free and equitable trade. The World Bank and the International Monetary Fund were created at a time when the conventional idea was that foreign aid was effective in promoting economic development in countries in difficulty. However, to contribute to reconstruction and development in post-war Europe, the Marshall Plan did not, at that time, grant European countries loans bearing conditions, but provided quick funding to address balance of payment problems to be able to promote and carry out the effective importation of goods and services indispensable to the daily needs of the countries affected by the war. The proof is that the World Bank delivered only four loans for the reconstruction of Europe, which cover a total of $497 million, while the Marshall Plan delivered $41.3 billion. (memoireonline.com) It was the United States through the Marshall Plan, rather than the World Bank, which was therefore the main driving force behind the reconstruction of Europe, even if that was strategic to deter the spread of Communism in Europe. Instead of using loans with strict conditions, African countries could find sustainable means for their reconstruction efforts, if the West is sincerely committed to free trade without political interference, and this could be considered as a form of partial contribution to Africa's reparation of the effects of the slave trade, Colonialism and apartheid.

The objectives set out in Article 1 of the IMF Articles of Agreement have therefore not been truly honoured, which supports the views of the critics that the mission of the Bretton Woods institutions is to strengthen the political, and socio-economic hegemony of the West on developing countries, particularly Sub-Saharan African countries. This is done by imposing conditions in the form of monetary and fiscal austerities. In addition, as we have noticed, the fact that the West contributes the major part of the resources of the IMF and the World Bank, and considering the decision-making process of these institutions, puts them under its politico-economic influence, especially that of the United States, which alone pays a quarter of the resources of the institutions individually.

Africa is aware that the IMF and the World Bank influence or even dominate its economic and political programmes through their Structural Adjustment Programme. In 1987, at the first international conference on the debt of the African continent, the

Organisation of African Trade Union Unity (OATUU)[41] called for the total cancellation of Africa's debt. Seven years earlier, the Lagos Plan of Action was adopted by African leaders. However, the Washington Consensus through the Elliot Berg[42] report of the World Bank in collaboration with the Fund, was accused of hampering its implementation by imposing the Structural Adjustment Programme on developing countries in exchange for its assistance.

Taking into account their disciplinary requirements in terms of fiscal and monetary policies, it is very difficult to defend the policies of the IMF and the World Bank vis-à-vis African reparation. They surely relieve the economic and financial problems of developing countries temporarily, but they equally impose sanctions on the countries that do not comply with their conditions, regardless of the reason for non-compliance and the social or economic costs of the sanctions, which might exceed the expected results. However, the World Bank is now trying to distinguish itself a little by becoming more aware of socio-economic variations and the impact of the Structural Adjustment Programme on developing countries.

---

[41]OATUU was founded in1973 in Addis Ababa, Ethiopia, at the initiative of the Organisation of African Unity to replace the All-African Trade Union Federation (AATUF), founded in 1961 and the African Trade Union Confederation (ATUC), founded in 1962. Members of OATUU include some 50 African trade unions, the South African Congress of Trade Unions and the National Union of Namibian Workers. Its objectives are to remain independent of other international labour organisations, to build trade union unity on the African continent, to coordinate the work of national trade unions as well as to support the interests of the African working class. Its headquarters are in Accra, Ghana.

[42] The Elliot Berg report entitled Accelerated Development in Sub-Saharan Africa, was prepared by Elliot Berg for the World Bank in 1981.

There are other unfavourable consequences that IMF policies seem to ignore and which represent a problem to mostly African Member States. Too many taxes and low wages weaken the economy, as they are likely to create popular dissatisfaction, brain drain, strikes and even uprisings. Unemployment and low wages, we have seen, sharply reduce demand for goods and services, and slow the process of production and consumption as well as investment, triggering a vicious cycle, which mostly leads the country concerned into recession. The IMF and World Bank should take into account the existence and essence of different economic cultures, and must not overlook the fact that economics as a social science is subject to fluctuations. In 1986, riots broke out in Zambia following an increase of 120% on the price of food in the country. The President blamed the austerity measures and conditions attached to structural adjustment loans. The same type of riots broke out in other African countries such as Mozambique in 2010, Malawi in 2011...

Some Western countries, such as Portugal, Spain, Italy, and especially Greece, have now realised the economic and financial troubles generated by the austerity measures of the Structural Adjustment Programme of the International Monetary Fund and the Bank. The IMF and the World Bank are essential, because they assist developing countries when there are few or no similar institutions to respond to their economic and financial needs. However, these institutions, in a position of near-monopoly, impose monetary and fiscal programmes and disciplinary measures on governments they consider disorderly, even if their requirements are unpleasant and have serious social and economic repercussions. Their interventions in African countries would contribute more constructively to African reparation if they paid more attention to the socio-economic variations and effects of their Structural Adjustment Programmes.

Conclusion

The Bretton Woods institutions were created at the beginning of the 1940s to promote international cooperation, free trade in goods and services globally as a means of ensuring the safety, stability and development of the international socio-economic systems after the devastating effects of the Great Depression of the 1930s and consequently those of World War II in the 1940s. They contributed to the promotion of development of the entire African continent in their own ways. However, their structures and functioning have been severely criticised for having contributed to, and even accelerated, the marginalisation of Sub-Saharan Africa. Their operations tend not to comply satisfactorily with the fundamental principles of free and equitable international trade that have been their raison d'être, consequently making Africa a victim of their systems. The Bretton Woods institutions have all contributed to the implementation of the economic policies defined by the Washington Consensus that as we have outlined, have engendered serious problems in Africa.

Within the WTO, the United States and the European Union made the Agreement on Agriculture unfavourable to Sub-Saharan Africa. There are political reasons for Western leaders to accord subsidies to their farmers, but the subsidies create an atmosphere of unfair trade because they affect the business of numerous farmers and their families. The Agreement on Trade-Related Aspects of Intellectual Property Rights (TRIPS), protecting copyrights and patents is also disadvantageous to Africa, especially the patents on medicine that require a minimum period of twenty (20) years before reproducing the same drugs even in generic forms. If patents encourage research and innovation, in our case the pharmaceutical sector, they reinforce the inequalities between Africa and developed countries. Intellectual property rights might be justified from the point of view of commercial law, however, they deny the sick access to medicines and effective treatment, and hence affect many people in Africa especially South Africa where the rate of the population affected by HIV/AIDS is alarming.

The Doha Development Agenda of the WTO was important, because it had multiple implications for Africa and the world economy at large. The success of the Doha Round would not only reduce tariffs and subsidies, but would also enable producers in both the agriculture and manufacturing sectors in developing countries to compete with other producers, eventually leading to global economic development, and thereby reducing poverty. Once developing countries have the opportunity to fairly compete in international trade, economic stability and growth will normally follow.

However, liberalisation of trade in services, reduction of barriers to trade in manufactured goods and the agreement on rules governing intellectual property rights which has been essential to Africa, especially concerning generic medicine, are key issues that have not been addressed in the recent Bali negotiations; yet Bali was a follow-up of the Doha Round. Also the Bali package for Least Developed Countries (LDC) instead of binding commitments, contains best endeavours, only reiterating the commitment of Member States to providing duty-free quota-free market access to LDCs, which might not be effective for lack of total coverage amongst other reasons.

The IMF and the World Bank have made important contributions to the international financial architecture and to socio-economic development, especially in Africa. The IMF has a tremendous effect on the global economy in its fundamental role of endeavouring to avoid dysfunctional adjustments when the balance of payments of a country is negative, that is to say when it does not have sufficient reserves to carry on trading with the rest of the world at the current rate of exchange. With its almost universal membership of 188 countries, the IMF is the main multilateral organisation to promote international macro-economic stability. It fulfils this mandate through surveillance of the financial and monetary situations of its Member States and the world economy at large, financially and technically providing assistance and advisory services to Member States to overcome major balance of payment problems. After the 1970s, the IMF adopted a new role in addressing the problems of poverty and promoting development in developing countries. Economic crises in the late 1970s and early 80s, as well as the recent United States subprime mortgage crisis that led to the financial crisis and subsequent recession beginning in 2008, have enormously hampered efforts of African reparation. What is remarkable is that the economic crisis of the 1970s paved the way for these financial institutions to intervene directly in Sub-Saharan African economies.

The Fund and the Bank therefore grant loans to African countries, like others in economic difficulties, to enable them to solve their problems of balance of payment and lack of competitiveness. These loans however have been linked with the imposition of certain restrictive measures on borrowing countries, usually the Structural Adjustment Programme, which under normal circumstances should be negotiated and prepared with national authorities, but in reality it is imposed on them by the IMF and the Bank, through directives and conditioning. Normally, the Fund should hold consultations with governments concerned, but they actually make unilateral decisions. Through these directives, the IMF requires countries seeking its intervention to apply a purely neo-liberal economic programme, as stipulated in the Washington Consensus. Sub-Saharan African countries, amongst others, are thence forced to comply with this programme and they end up being overloaded with debts and consequently plunged into more economic problems. The Structural Adjustment Programme led to the privatisation of key State-owned enterprises in the economies of most African countries, widespread trade liberalisation leading often to the indiscriminate opening of African markets to foreign, mostly Western entrepreneurs and a reduction in public spending. The devaluation of national currencies, which accordingly makes domestic products more attractive to foreign buyers and helps encourage exports and foreign investment in the country, is often recommended, but devaluation also makes the cost of living more expensive at the local level, especially if incomes do not increase at the same rate. The architects of the Washington Consensus developed the programme with the idea that stability in the macro-economic sector is the key to creating jobs and reducing income disparities and poverty in a general perspective. However, even if the idea behind this theory is obvious and even if IMF interventions allow an improvement of the economic situation of the countries concerned, they often cause complications. Public enterprises that occupy strategic positions such as energy and water, railways and telecommunications service providers are privatised, and eventually most often end up in the hands of foreign companies, which do not have the same social vocations as national companies. As the privatisation of enterprises has often been in favour of foreign (Western) countries and their multinationals, the products and services generated by these businesses are mostly afforded only by the wealthy minority, if they are consumed locally at all. The fierce nature of competition in business and trade mostly leads to bankruptcy of many domestic enterprises, under the Structural Adjustment Programme, resulting in unemployment and a loss of purchasing power, thereby further weakening national economies. The removal of price control, the freezing of wages and the artificial redundancies of millions of workers in the framework of the Structural Adjustment Programme aggravates unemployment. The Structural Adjustment Programme therefore has the effect of contributing to increasing poverty in Africa, thereby intensifying the inequalities between Sub-Saharan Africa and the rest of the world, especially the West. While some Africans are not totally against liberalisation, some consider that:

> ...trade liberalisation has to go with a development agenda. You cannot liberalise trade, when the people in the country are not able to develop their own

> industries, develop their own small enterprises, employ people in the country, [...] What the IMF is doing is to get a few services and infrastructure going and they say they have done something. That's short-term, it's not long-term. (Personal interview, 20 June 2007)

These policies, however, affect the sovereignty of national economies because they limit the capacities of the States concerned to embark on appropriate and constructive economic programmes. When the parliaments of countries concerned become simple observers and almost statues of economic decisions concerning their countries, we might ask about the essence of elections and democratic processes and institutions. The economic programmes and budget of the Member States and most of the decisions of their governments are a means of redistributing national resources. However through these conditions, the IMF and the World Bank intervene in virtually all sectors of public life in African countries without being accountable to anyone. These conditions force African countries amongst others to prejudicially endure the problems of their external balances, even if they are caused by exogenous factors such as international financial crises and a fall in commodity prices.

The General Agreement on Trade in Services (GATS), which is about liberalising services, has created a lot of public discontent and reaction in Europe, because it threatens jobs and the survival of the public service itself. It was the same in Africa, where the liberalisation of services was often one of the conditions imposed by the Structural Adjustment Programme of the IMF and the World Bank.

The share of loans from the IMF and the World Bank in the total public debt of African countries has grown to an unbearable level. And according to this African diplomat:

> Most of the people attached to the projects as consultants come from these countries and half the money of the projects is spent on vehicles and salaries for the consultants they have chosen themselves. So who are you helping? If you say you give 90 million loan to a country and you take 40 million to pay salaries for consultants and cars, you might as well say I give 50 million... It's like giving with one hand and taking back what you have given with the other hand. (Personal interview, 20 June 2007)

The excessive debt of African countries, as we have already observed, has affected economic growth on the continent. The result of the strategies of the IMF, the World Bank and the World Trade Organisation, is an increase in inequality of income that has more than doubled worldwide since the 1960s, while the gap between rich and poor countries continues to increase to the disadvantage of poor countries. In fact, most strategies of the IMF have failed, notably in Africa. The 1980s, considered as the "lost decade" in Africa in terms of economic growth, is concrete proof of this situation. The People's Republic of China has experienced strong and steady growth over the past twenty years; paradoxically it is one of the few countries, and the major one, to have carried out its economic policies almost independently with very little relationship with the IMF or the Bank. Since 1981, China has used IMF credits only twice, in 1981 and in 1986, and the credits under these arrangements have been fully repaid. The redefinition of the policies of liberalisation and privatisation, and the reformulation of the overall methods of functioning of the IMF and the World Bank is a necessity for Africa to participate equally in the principles of globalisation, fair trade and development.

Joseph Stiglitz has pointed out the unsuitability of the policies of the Bretton Woods institutions to developing countries arguing that:

> The Keynesian orientation of the IMF, which emphasized market failures and the role for government in job creation, was replaced by the free market mantra of the 1980s, part of a new "Washington Consensus"- a consensus between the IMF, the World Bank and the U.S. Treasury about the "right" policy for developing countries – that signalled a radically different approach to economic development and stabilization. (Stiglitz 16)

This reminds us about the views of several other observers including Jesse Helms, Chairman of the Foreign Affairs Committee of the U.S. Senate, that the United Nations and other international institutions such as the WTO, the World Bank and the IMF are institutions that serve as politico-economic imperial instruments to safeguard and increase the dominance of the West, notably that of the United States, of other countries.

The International Monetary Fund is not rationally and effectively operating to avoid dysfunctional adjustments in its Member States' balance of payments; and the World Trade Organisation is neither fairly mediating trade disputes, nor genuinely promoting free trade and economic and social development in accordance with the principle of democracy and equity. Their initial collective goal was to achieve international cooperation in solving international problems of an economic, social, or humanitarian nature. However, this has evolved over time as Joseph Stiglitz put it. Otherwise they would have sincerely done as much in Africa and other developing countries as the Marshall Plan did in Europe after World War II, given what the West owes Africa, even if that would come with some motivation like that of the Marshall Plan whose strategic interest to a certain point was to combat Communism in Europe, or like China's operative aids in Africa whose motivation was to strategically get access to Africa's natural resources especially oil.

The African Union has not remained inert. Since 1980, its predecessor, the Organisation of African Unity (OAU) has proposed a series of measures to promote economic development on the continent, including the Lagos Plan of Action (LPA) that envisaged socio-economic development in Africa based on cooperation, economic integration and self-reliance. It even established the modalities of an African Economic Community to be created around the year 2000.[43]

---

[43] The OAU Heads of State and Government signed the Treaty establishing the African Economic Community (AEC) during the 27th Ordinary Session of the Assembly in Abuja, Nigeria in June 1991. Since May 1994, the OAU has been operating on the basis of the Charter of OAU and the Treaty of AEC, and the organisation was officially referred to as the OAU/AEC. The aim of the AEC is to promote economic, social and cultural development as well as the economic integration of Africa as a means of increasing the continent's self-sufficiency and endogenous development as well as creating a framework for development through the mobilisation of human and material resources. AEC also aims at promoting co-operation and development of Africans with a view to raising the standard of living of the peoples of Africa, maintaining economic stability and

However, the Lagos Plan of Action that raised a lot of hope and aspirations, coincided with the Structural Adjustment Programmes (SAP), and could not be implemented due to lack of resources, and therefore was hampered by the policies of the World Bank and the IMF. Efforts by the African Union continue today; the African Union has established the African Monetary Fund (AMF), which is stipulated in article 19 of its Constitutive Act, through the harmonisation of monetary zones and the creation of two other African Union financial institutions, namely the African Central Bank (ACB) and the African Investment Bank (AIB). The African Investment Bank aims at fostering economic growth and accelerating economic integration in Africa in accordance with the objectives of the African Union. As for the African Central Bank, that was created following the 1991 Abuja Treaty and reiterated by the 1999 Sirte Declaration, its aim is to build a common monetary policy and facilitate the creation of an African currency to foster the acceleration of economic integration on the continent. A new plan to help revive the economy of the African continent, the New Partnership for Africa's Development, (NEPAD) adopted at the OAU summit in Lusaka, Zambia, in July 2001, has been based on the same perspectives, even though some observers criticised the initial project of NEPAD as being based on the Bretton Woods model, which is a network of collaboration with the international community,

---

establishing a peaceful relationship amongst Member States. The Treaty of the AEC (commonly known as the Abuja Treaty) came into force in May 1994, after the requisite numbers of Member States ratified it. Its implementation is a process that would be done in 6 stages by 2028, i.e., over 34 years.

especially Western countries and their multilateral organisations. NEPAD is now a programme of the African Union (AU) that aims to build the capacity of Africa to actively and effectively participate in the global economy and politics, accelerate the empowerment of women, eradicate poverty and promote sustainable growth and development in Africa.

In the context of international trade, the approach suggested by David Ricardo in his theory of comparative advantages clearly indicates the conditions under which specialisation and free trade should take place for the benefit of all. The major condition, according to Ricardo, for free trade to benefit all parties is an atmosphere of perfect competition, without political pressure. Also, the geographic location and economic culture of the world when Ricardo stated his theory was different and still radically different from those of contemporary Africa. In addition, Ricardo took the West as an absolute benchmark of his theory without any consideration of Africa. Moreover African countries have not yet seemingly satisfied the requirements to independently and effectively insert their economies into the world market in the perspective of globalisation. This has several attributes, mainly the impact of slavery and Colonialism, and post-colonial relations, in a political and economic context, but equally, as we have already outlined, the systems of government in Africa. All these phenomena make African economies very weak, thereby affecting the production as well as the export of manufactured goods and services, and then reducing the volume of foreign investment and consequently adversely affecting African countries on the capital markets.

We have said that the Structural Adjustment Programme in its economic and political dimensions usually requires the disengagement of the State in the economy as a public sector, in favour of the private sector; which usually has the consequence of destroying the distributive role and capacity of the State, hence its social vocation. Another problem of the African continent, however, is that many African governments have not been able to engage their people in concrete development initiatives in order to realise and exert their potential creativity. Also, African policy-makers should better integrate aspects of African cultures in their development programmes. The programmes of these institutions and the inadequacy of aspects of cultural and economic renaissance within African perspectives and values in the development programmes of African countries at national level are sources of failure of strategies, which push the continent more into debt and insecurity, in spite of its enormous resources. These are actually the negative aspects that some African nationalists continue to combat, but have been ineffective due to several barriers including those being erected and guarded by Imperialism, but most importantly by the unpatriotic attitude of some Africans themselves, who compromise their national developments for their personal positions and well-being. All these deficiencies are compounded by the policies of the Bretton Woods institutions. The combined effects of this inability or weakness of the State, typical of Africa, and the policies carried out by these institutions, and especially the adverse lack of African Cultural values represent major obstacles to African development. Therefore, in spite of more than

50 years of independence and statehood, the average African is not apt in strengthening the capacity to govern and participate in government to implement economic and social projects and policies in the long term, without soliciting the intervention of foreign governments: the West, China, Japan, Taiwan, Turkey... and their financial institutions. Africa ought also to have ways of funding its own development programmes, and adopt the strategies of ECOWAS, which has been based on community levy to raise resources for the bulk of its activities. Thence to effectively carry out concrete reconstruction programmes, Africa must liberate itself of this dependency syndrome and diminish its reliance on external aid. It must also strengthen its own domestic policies and hold fast to taking common positions especially on key issues within the United Nations and other international organisation. The African peoples must re-establish confidence in their own capacities and values and capabilities and carry out their development programmes with common vision and common discourse to be respected, and listened to, not merely considered when its votes are needed; but the peoples must first of all re-establish self-discipline and self-respect in their own societies. In that way the continent can further kick away the artificial barriers of colonial cultures, namely Anglophone, Francophone and Lusophone, and develop and promote the genuine aspects and factors of their sustainable development: their own values and cultures.

Bibliography

Primary sources

Personal interviews

Personal interview, 20 June 2007.

Personal interview, 15 July 2007

Archives of the African Union

AHG/Res.130 (XIX) Resolution on the Establishment of a Special Fund for Africa, Assembly of Heads of State and government, Twentieth Ordinary Session 12 – 15 November 1984 Addis Ababa, Ethiopia.

AHG/Res.131 (XIX) Resolution on the Inter-African Economic Co-operation and Integration, Assembly of Heads of State and government, Twentieth Ordinary Session 12 – 15 November 1984 Addis Ababa, Ethiopia.

AHG/Res.190 (XXVI) Resolution on the Establishment of the African Economic Community, Assembly of Heads of State and government, Twenty-sixth Ordinary Session 9 – 11 July 1990 Addis Ababa, Ethiopia.

AHG/Decl.2 (XXXVI) Lome Declaration, Assembly of Heads of State and government, Thirty-Sixth Ordinary Session/Fourth Ordinary Session of the African Economic Community 10-12 July, 2000 Lome, Togo.

AHG/Decl.5 (XXXVI) Declaration on the Framework for an OAU response to unconstitutional changes of government, Assembly of Heads of State and government, Thirty-Sixth Ordinary Session/Fourth Ordinary Session of the African Economic Community 10-12 July, 2000 Lome, Togo.

Assembly/AU/Decl. 2 (V) Sirte Declaration on the Reform of the United Nations, Assembly of the African Union, Fifth Ordinary Session 4 – 5 July 2005 Sirte, Libya.

Assembly/AU/Resolution.1 (V) Resolution on the United Nations Reform: Security Council Assembly of the African Union, Fifth Ordinary Session 4 – 5 July 2005 Sirte, Libya.

Assembly/AU/Dec.166 (IX) Decision on the Protocol on Relations between the African Union and the Regional Economic Communities

Ext/EX.CL/2 (VII) The Common African Position on the Proposed Reform of the United Nations: *"The Ezulwini Consensus"* Executive

Council, 7th Extraordinary Session 7- 8 March 2005, Addis Ababa, Ethiopia.

Organisation of African Unity. OAU Charter. 25 May 1963, Addis Ababa, Ethiopia.

African Union. Constitutive Act of the African Union, 11 JULY, 2000, Lome, Togo.

Archives of the United Nations Organisation

UN. ECOSOC Resolution 2002/1 Ad hoc advisory group on African countries emerging from conflict 23rd plenary meeting, 15 July 2002.

UNTS XVI, United Nations, Charter of the United Nations, 1945, 1 UNTS XVI.

AG/10418) Rapport de débat sur l'élargissement du Conseil à l'Assemblée générale, 47e& 48e séances plénières, le 11 novembre 2005.

A/CONF.189/12. Report of the World Conference against Racism, Racial Discrimination, Xenophobia and Related Intolerance, Durban, 31 August- 8 September 2001.

S/RES/462 (1980) International peace and security, 9 January 1980.

S/RES/308 (1972) Request of the Organization of African Unity concerning the holding of meetings of the Security Council in an African Capital (General Assembly Resolution 2863 (XXVI), para. 2), 19 January 1972.

S/RES/311 (1972) The Question of race conflict in South Africa resulting from the policies of apartheid of the Government of the Republic of South Africa, 4 February 1972.

RES/190(1964) Question relating to the policies of apartheid of the Government of the Republic of South Africa. Resolution 190 (1964) Adopted by the Security Council on 9 June 1964.

S/RES/110 (1955) Question of reviewing the Charter of the UN Resolution of 14 December 1955 (s/3509)

S/RES/1631 (2005) Cooperation between the United Nations and regional organizations in maintaining international peace and security, Resolution 1631 (2005) Resolution 1631 (2005) Adopted by the Security Council at its 5282nd meeting, on 17 October 2005.

S/RES/1625 (2005) Threats to international peace and security (Security Council Summit 2005), Resolution 1625 (2005) Adopted by the Security Council at its 5261st meeting, on 14 September 2005.

S/RES/1624 (2005) Threats to international peace and security (Security Council Summit 2005), Resolution 1624 (2005) Adopted by the Security Council at its 5261st meeting, on 14 September 2005.

S/RES/1631 (2005) Cooperation between the United Nations and regional organizations in maintaining international peace and security, Resolution 1631 (2005) Adopted by the Security Council at its 5282nd meeting, on 17 October 2005.

S/RES/1318 (2000) Effective role for the Security Council in the maintenance of international peace and security, particularly in Africa, Resolution 1318 (2000) Adopted by the Security Council at its 4194th meeting, on 7 September 2000.

S/RES/919 (1994) South Africa Resolution 919 (1994) Adopted by the Security Council at its 3379th meeting, 25 May 1994.

S/RES/462 (1980) UN Security Council, Security Council Resolution 462 (1980) Adopted by the Security Council at its 2190th meeting, on 9 January 1980.

Resolution 2002/1 ECOSOC Ad hoc advisory group on African countries emerging from conflict 23rd plenary meeting, 15 July 2002.

Archives of the International Monetary Fund.

The International Monetary Fund. *World economic outlook: a survey by the staff of the International Monetary Fund.* Washington, D.C.: The International Monetary Fund, 1980.

International Monetary Fund. *World Economic Outlook (WEO), International Monetary Fund* Washington, D.C.: The International Monetary Fund, September 2006.

International Monetary Fund. *Regional economic outlook: Sub-Saharan Africa -* Washington, D.C.: International Monetary Fund, May 2006.

International Monetary Fund. *Integrating Poor Countries into the World Trading System* Washington, D.C: International Monetary Fund, April 2006.

International Monetary Fund. *Promoting Growth in Sub-Saharan Africa: Learning What Works,* Washington, D.C: International Monetary Fund, 2000.

The International Monetary Fund, the United Nations, the World Bank, and the Organisation for Economic Co-operation and Development. *A Better World for All Progress towards the international development goals,* Washington, D.C.: International Monetary Fund, 2000.

IMF, Articles of Agreement of the International Monetary Fund, Bretton Woods, New Hampshire, July 22, 1944.

Archives of the World Bank Group

World Bank. World Development Report 2005: A Better Investment Climate for Everyone, Washington, D.C.: World Bank, September 2004.

World Bank. World Development Report 2002: Building Institutions for Markets. Washington, D.C.: World Bank, September 2001.

World Bank. African Development Indicators 2005: From the World Bank Africa Database. Washington, D.C.: World Bank, July 2005.

World Bank. African Development Indicators 2004: Drawn from the World Bank Africa Database. Washington, D.C.: World Bank, March 2004.

World Bank. Africa Development Indicators 2006: From the World Bank Africa Database. Washington, D.C.: World Bank, September 2006,

World Bank. The Uruguay Round: Widening and deepening the world trading system, Washington, D.C.: World Bank, October 1995.

The World Bank, IBRD Articles of Agreement (as amended effective June 27, 2012

World Bank. World Development Report 2003: Sustainable Development in a Dynamic World: Transforming Institutions, Growth, and Quality of Life August 2002, Oxford University Press.

Archives of the World Trade Organisation.

WT/MIN (01)/DEC/1 DOHA WTO Ministerial 2001: Ministerial Declaration. WT/MIN (01)/DEC/1 Adopted in Doha, 14 November 2001.

WT/MIN (01)/DEC/2 Declaration on the TRIPS Agreement and Public Health, Ministerial Conference, Fourth Session, Doha, 9 - 14 November 2001.

WTO. Uruguay Round Agreement, Marrakesh Declaration of 15 April 1994,

WT/MIN (13)/DEC Bali Ministerial Declaration and decisions adopted on 7 December 2013. WT/MIN (13)/31WT/L/906. Trips non-violation and situation complaints Ministerial Decision of 7 December 2013.

WT/MIN (13)/34WT/L/909 Aid for trade Ministerial Decision of 7 December 2013. WT/MIN (13)/35WT/L/910 Trade and Transfer of Technology, Ministerial Decision of 7 December 2013.

WT/MIN (13)/36WT/L/911 Agreement on trade and facilitation Ministerial Decision of 7 December 2013.

WT/MIN (13)/39WT/L/914 Understanding on tariff rate quota administration provisions of agricultural products, as defined in article 2 of the agreement on agriculture Ministerial Decision of 7 December 2013.

The General Agreement on Tariffs and Trade (GATT 1947)

Secondary sources

Books

B.

Budhoo, Davidson. ed Kevin Danaher, *IMF / World Bank Wreak Havoc on Third World*, USA, South End Press, 1994.

Burke, Edmund. 2000. *On Empire, Liberty and Reform: Speeches and Letters*. Ed. David Bromwich. New Haven: Yale University Press.

D.

Davidson, Basil. *Africa in modern history: the search for a new society*. London: Allen Lane, 1978.

Davidson, Basil. *The growth of African civilisation: a study of West Africa (1000-1800)*. London: Longman, 1965.

Dickson, A Mungazi. *The Mind of Black Africa*. Connecticut: Westport, 1996.

Dingnan, Peter. *The United States and Africa: a history*. Cambridge: Cambridge University Press, 1984.

F.

Fanon Frantz. *Les damnés de la terre*, Paris : Éditions la Découverte, 1968.

Fanon, Frantz. *Peau Noire Masques Blancs*, Paris : Seuil, 1968.

Ferro, Marc ed. *Le livre noire du colonialisme XVIe – XXIe siècle : de l'extermination à la repentance*, Paris, éditions Robert Laffont, 2003.

Fleurence, Olivier. *La Réforme du Conseil de Sécurité : l'État du débat depuis la fin de la Guerre Froide*. Bruxelles, Établissements Émile Bruylant, 2000.

G.

Gann L H, Duignan Peter. *Colonialism in Africa 1870 – 1960* Volumes 1 and 2, New York, Cambridge University Press, 1969.

Gandhi, Leela. *Postcolonial Theory: A Critical Introduction*. New York: Columbia University Press, 1988.

Gordon, April A. and Donald L. Gordon, eds. *Understanding Contemporary Africa.* 2nd ed. Boulder, CO: Lynne Rienner Publishers, 1996.

H.

Hargreaves, John D. *Decolonization in Africa*, London: Longman Group UK. 1990.

Huntington, Samuel P. *Political Order in Changing Society.* New Haven and London, Yale University Press, 1968.

K.

Kennedy, Paul. *The Rise and fall of Great Powers*, London: Fontana Press, 1988.

Kitchen, Lexington, Helen, Mass, ed. *Africa: from mystery to maze.* Toronto: Lexington Books, 1978.

Killingray, David. *Africa and the Second World War.* London: Macmillan, 1986.

Kent, John. *The Internalization of Colonialism: Britain, France and Black Africa.* 1939-1956. Oxford: Oxford University Press, 1992.

King, Martin Luther Jr. *Stride Toward Freedom*, New York: Harper and Row, 1958.

L.

Lancaster, Carol. *So Much To Do, So Little Done*, Chicago: University of Chicago Press, 1999.

Legum, Colin. *Africa; a Handbook to the Continent.* New York: Praeger, 1962.

Loomba, Ania. *Colonialismpostcolonialism.* London, New York: Routledge, 1998.

Lynn, Martin. *Commerce and Economic Change in West Africa: the palm oil trade in the nineteenth century.* Cambridge: Cambridge University Press, 1997.

Lugan, Bernard. *Afrique: de la colonisation philanthropique à la recolonisation humanitaire*, Paris : Christian de Bartillat, 1995.

N.

Ndegwa, Philip. *Africa's Development Crisis.* London: Heinemann, 1988.

Ngugi wa Thiong'o. *Decolonising the Mind: The Politics of Language in African Literature.* London: J. Currey; Portsmouth, N.H. : Heinemann, 1986.

Ngugi wa Thiong'o. *Moving the Centre: The Struggle for Cultural Freedoms.* London: J. Currey; Portsmouth, N.H.: Heinemann, 1993. .

Nkurumah, Kwame. *Towards Colonial Freedom: Africa in the struggle against world imperialism.* London: Panaf, 1979.

Nkurumah, Kwame. *Class Struggle in Africa.* London: Panaf, 1970.

Nkrumah, Kwame. *Neo-Colonialism: The Last Stage of Imperialism*, London: Heinemann, 1965.

Nkrumah, Kwame. *Challenge of the Congo. A Case Study of Foreign Pressures in an Independent State*, London: Panaf, 1966.

Nkrumah, Kwame. *Handbook of Revolutionary Warfare*, London: Panaf, 1968.

Nkrumah, Kwame. *Revolutionary Path*, London: Panaf, 1973.

O.

Oliver, Roland Anthony. *Africa in the Iron Age: C. 500 BC to AD 1400*. Cambridge, London, New York: Cambridge University Press, 1975.

Omer-Cooper J D. *The Making of Modern Africa*. New York: Humanities Press, 1968.

P.

Pitts, Jennifer. *A Turn Toward Empire: The Rise of Imperial Liberalism in Britain and France*. Princeton and Oxford: Princeton University Press, 2005.

R.

Ravenhill, John. *Africa in Economic Crisis*. London: Macmillan, 1986.

Reader, John. *Africa: A Biography of the Continent*. London: Hamish Hamilton, 1997, 840p.

Ricardo, David, *On the Principles of Political Economy and Taxation, 3rd edition*, London: John Murray, 1821.

Rodney, Walter. *How Europe Underdeveloped Africa*, Washington D.C.: Howard University Press, 1982.

S.

Shepherd, George W. Ed. Ved P. Nanda, George W. Shepherd, and Eileen McCarthy-Arnolds. *The African Right to Development and Adjustment: World Policy and the Debt Crisis*. Westport, CT: Greenwood Press, 1993.

T.

Thornton, John L. *Africa and Africans in the making of the Atlantic world: 1400-1800* 2nd ed. Cambridge, MA: Cambridge University Press, 1998.

Periodicals

Colette, Elise. "L'Afrique est une priorité", *Jeune Afrique l'intelligent*, n° 2198.43e année, (février – mars 2003): 64.

Constantin, F. Constantin, B., "Perspectives africaines et bouleversements internationaux", *Politique Africaine, "l'Afrique autrement"*, n°39 (février 1990): 59.

Lucien Manokou, "L'Afrique et le Conseil de Sécurité de l'ONU (1946-1990)." *Guerres mondiales et conflits contemporains*, Paris, n° 196, décembre 1999 : 10.

Maja, Steven. "Distilling the vision of an African Union." *Southern African Political & Economic Monthly (SAPEM)* Vol.14, N° 6, (2001): 5-6.
Manima, Norah. "Conflits africains: le lourd tribute économique", *La nouvelle Afrique*, n°6 (février – mars 2003): 42-45.

Web pages
ACALAN, "Terms of Reference for the harmonisation of the Fulfulde, Hausa and Mandenkan Vehicular Cross-border Languages, 14-16 July 2010." 10 Feb. 2013. <http://www.acalan.org/eng/accueil/accueil.php>
Apollos O. Nwauwa. "Concepts of Democracy and Democratization in Africa Revisited." *Paper presented at the Fourth Annual Kent State University Symposium on Democracy* 15 Aug. 2013.
<http://upress.kent.edu/Nieman/Concepts_of_Democracy.htm>
Bureau, Jean-Christophe, Decreux, Yvan, Gohin, Alexandre. "La libéralisation des échanges agricoles dans le cadre de l'OMC: impact économique." 15 Sept. 2013.
<http://www.insee.fr/fr/ffc/docs_ffc/ref/agrifra07k.pdf)>.
Driscoll, David D. "The IMF and the World Bank: How Do They Differ?" 12 June 2013.
<https://www.imf.org/external/pubs/ft/exrp/differ/differ.htm>
Bubulle, "Commentaire CIJ, essais nucléaires 1974." 10 Oct. 2013.
<http://www.juriste-en-herbe.com/droit-international-public/270-commentaire-cij-essais-nucleaires-1974>
Le Droit suisse. "Droit International Public: L'affaire Nicaragua-USA." 05 Feb. 2013. <http://www.format-prod.com/droit-etudiants/dip-usa-nicaragua.html>
UNESCO. "Bureau de l'UNESCO à Dakar." 13 May 2013.
<http://www.unesco.org/new/fr/dakar/about-this-office/>.
Houtart, François. "L'échec des politiques d'ajustement structurel de la Banque mondiale par (mai 2002) 02 Nov. 2013.
<http://www.cetri.be/spip.php?article420>
IDA, "ABCs of IDA—Thematic and Country Results." 10 Jan. 2014.
<http://www.worldbank.org/ida/ida_abc.html>
Malingumu Syosyo, Crispin. "Les interventions des institutions de Bretton Woods en Afrique : contraintes et limites. " 15 Jan. 2014.
<http://www.congoforum.be/fr/economiedetail.asp?subitem=31&id=23917&economie=selected>
Defarges, Philippe Moreau. "La Reforme de l'ONU ? Obsedante et Impossible." 12 Feb. 2014. <http://www.afri-ct.org/IMG/pdf/67_Moreau_Defarges.pdf>

Lecoutre, Delphine. "Des voix du Sud au Conseil de sécurité : L'Afrique et la réforme des Nations unies." juillet 2005. 18 Feb. 2014. <http://www.monde-diplomatique.fr/2005/07/LECOUTRE/12441>

Ramdoo, Isabelle. "9th WTO Ministerial in Bali: Trade deal struck, but what implications for geopolitics?" 06 Feb. 2014. <http://www.ecdpm-talkingpoints.org/9th-wto-ministerial-in-bali-trade-deal-struck-but-what-implications-for-geopolitics/>

Kanyimbo, Patrick, Calvin, Manduna. "Trade facilitation in the Bali Package: What's in it for Africa?" 06 Dec. 2013. <http://www.afdb.org/en/blogs/integrating-africa/post/trade-facilitation-in-the-bali-package-whats-in-it-for-africa-12698/>

"La France à l'ONU, Représentation permanent de la France auprès des Nations Unies à New York : La Réforme du Conseil de Sécurité des Nations Unies" 06 Aug. 2013. <http://www.franceonu.org/la-france-a-l-onu/dossiers-thematiques/reforme-de-l-onu/la-reforme-du-conseil-de-securite/article/la-reforme-du-conseil-de-securite>.

"Remarks by the President to the Joint Session of the Indian Parliament in New Delhi, India Parliament House, New Delhi, India." 08 Nov. 2010. <http://www.whitehouse.gov/the-press-office/2010/11/08/remarks-president-joint-session-indian-parliament-new-delhi-india>.

"The Common Agricultural Policy: A partnership between Europe and Farmers." 10 Nov. 2013. <http://ec.europa.eu/agriculture/cap-overview/2012_en.pdf>.

Georges-Henri Soutou, "La France et la creéation de l'ONU 1944-1946." 12 Aug. 2013. <http://www.diplomatie.gouv.fr/fr/IMG/pdf/ONU_gh_soutou.pdf>

Nations Unies. "L'Assemblée Générale Débat de la Réforme du Conseil de Sécurité, Assemblée générale, 47ᵉ & 48ᵉ séances plénières, matin & après-midi." 20 Dec. 2013. <http://www.un.org/News/fr-press/docs/2005/AG10418.doc.htm>

United Nations. "Remarks by Senator Jesse Helms to the United Nations Security Council." 10 Dec. 2013. <http://www.derechos.org/nizkor/impu/tpi/helms2.html>

OMC. "Structure, fonctionnement, buts. 10 Aug. 2013. <http://perso.fundp.ac.be/~cedes6/f5/gr4/Cb_OMC_strct_fonct_buts.htm>

The World Bank. "The World Bank's First Loan, May 9, 1947." 02 Feb 2014. <http://web.worldbank.org/WBSITE/EXTERNAL/EXTABOUTUS

/EXTARCHIVES/0,,contentMDK:20035704~pagePK:36726~piPK:36
092~menuPK:56273~theSitePK:29506,00.html>

Socialist alternative. "Part I: The IMF, the World Bank, and the Global
Economy." 15 Feb. 2014.
<http://www.socialistalternative.org/publications/imfwb/>

United Nations. "China supports UN Security Council reform,
November 9, 2010."
<http://www.un.org/News/Press/docs/2005/ga10368.doc.htm>

WTO. "Documents from the negotiating chairs, 21 April 2011." 10 Jan.
2014.
<http://www.wto.org/english/tratop_e/dda_e/chair_texts11_e/chair_te
xts11_e.htm>

UNDP. "The United Nations Development Programme in Africa." 29
Dec. 2013. <http://www.africa.undp.org/rba/en/home.html>

United Nations. "UN, ECOSOC MEMBERS." 10 Jan. 2014.
<http://www.un.org/en/ecosoc/about/members.shtml>

WTO. "The Doha Round." 15 Feb. 2014.
<http://www.wto.org/english/tratop_e/dda_e/dda_e.htm>

Féderation Internationale des Organisations de Travailleurs de la
Metallurgie. "Les propositions OMC NAMA sont mauvaises pour le
développement." 02 Jan. 2014.
<http://www.imfmetal.org/index.cfm?c=16364&l=5>

Laverie, Cedric. "La cohérence de la double conditionnalité des
institutions de Bretton Woods, *Université Paris X - D.E.A. de Droit des
Relations Economiques Internationales et Communautaires 2001*. 05 Dec. 2013.
<http://www.memoireonline.com/08/08/1499/m_coherence-double-
conditionnalite-institutions-bretton-woods4.html>

United Nations. "Role of the General Assembly." 16 Nov. 2013.
< https://www.un.org/en/peacekeeping/operations/rolega.shtml>

United Nations. "Role of the General Assembly." 15 Jan. 2013.
<https://www.un.org/en/peacekeeping/operations/rolega.shtml

"The Common Agricultural Policy: A partnership between Europe and
Farmers." 05 Dec. 2013. <http://ec.europa.eu/agriculture/cap-
overview/2012_en.pdf

IMF. "At a Glance - China and the IMF" 10 Jan. 2014.
<https://www.imf.org/external/country/chn/rr/glance.htm>

Nations Unies. "Groupes consultatifs spéciaux pour les pays africains qui
sortent d'un conflit. " 05 Dec. 2013.
<http://www.un.org/fr/ecosoc/adhocmech/conflict.shtml>

Davison Budhoo. "Third world traveller, IMF/World Bank Wreak Havoc on Third World." 16 Nov. 2013.
<http://www.thirdworldtraveler.com/IMF_WB/Budhoo_50YIE.html>
Zacharia, Janine. "U.S. Calls for Two More Permanent UN Council Seats." 08 Dec. 2013.
<http://www.bloomberg.com/apps/news?pid=newsarchive&sid=aFdg w208I7jc>
Nations Unies. "UNCTAD/SDTE/ECB/2005/1 Report: United Nations Conference on Trade and Development." Geneva, 31 Oct 2005. 20 Feb. 2014.
<http://unctad.org/en/Docs/sdteecb20051overview_en.pdf>
ECOFIN FINANCE. "IFC : un record de 4 milliards $ d'investissements en Afrique subsaharienne." 20 Feb. 2014.
<http://www.agenceecofin.com/investissement/3008-6451-ifc-un-record-de-4-milliards-d-investissements-en-afrique-subsaharienne>

Online Newspapers

Bobin, Frédéric. "Les BRICS haussent le ton sur la réforme de la Banque Mondiale et du FMI." *Le Monde*, 30 mars 2012. 10 Jan. 2013.
<http://www.lemonde.fr/international/article/2012/03/30/les-brics-haussent-le-ton-sur-la-reforme-de-la-banque-mondiale-et-du-fmi_1678145_3210.html>.
Geneste, Alexandra. "Les Nations unies appellent la France à "décoloniser" la Polynésie", Le *Monde*, 18 mai, 2013. 02 Feb. 2013.
<http://www.lemonde.fr/international/article/2013/05/18/les-nations-unies-appellent-la-france-a-decoloniser-la-polynesie_3316116_3210.html>
Grunberg, Isabelle. "Que faire du Fonds monétaire international?" *Le Monde diplomatique*, sept. 2000. 15 Jan. 2014. <http://www.monde-diplomatique.fr/2000/09/GRUNBERG/14172>
Mbaye, Sanou. "En finir avec la dépendance : Souhaitable union des économies africaines," *Le Monde diplomatique*, septembre 1995. 13 Sept. 2012. <http://www.monde-diplomatique.fr/1995/09/MBAYE/1731>.
Lacouture, Jean. "Bandung ou la fin de l'ère coloniale." avril 2005. 25 Jul. 2012.
<http://www.monde-diplomatique.fr/2005/04/LACOUTURE/12062>

La Croix, "La résolution 2085 de l'ONU sur le Mali." *La Croix*, 14 Jan 2013. 16 Jan. 2014. <http://www.la-croix.com/Actualite/Monde/La-resolution-2085-de-l-ONU-sur-le-Mali-_NG_-2013-01-14-898950>.

Pacific Magazine, "REGION: Cook Islands puts New Zealand citizenship first", *Pacific Magazine*, 14 June 2001. 20 Feb. 2014.

Stiglitz, Joseph. "The Insider: What I Learnt at the World Economic Crisis." *The New Republic*, Washington DC, 17 April 2000. 03 Dec. 2013. <http://sandovalhernandezj.people.cofc.edu/index_files/egl_20.pdf>.

Le Monde. "L'Inde et la France relancent leur partenariat stratégique." *Le Monde.fr avec AFP et Reuters*, 12 sept. 2005. 26 Feb. 2014. <http://www.lemonde.fr/asie-pacifique/article/2005/09/12/de-retour-aux-affaires-m-chirac-relance-le-partenariat-strategique-entre-l-inde-et-la-france_688394_3216.html>

Robinson, Mary, "Africa Needs Fair Trade, Not Charity." *Yale Global*, 23 Aug 2005. 18 Jan. 2014. <http://yaleglobal.yale.edu/content/africa-needs-fair-trade-not-charity-0>

Joseph Stiglitz. "The Insider: What I Learnt at the World Economic Crisis", *The New Republic*, Washington DC, 17 April 2000. 16 Aug. 2013. <http://sandovalhernandezj.people.cofc.edu/index_files/egl_20.pdf>.

Libération. "Jim Yong Kim, nouveau président de la Banque Mondiale. " *Libération (Economie)*, 16 avril 2012. 10 Jan. 2014. <http://www.liberation.fr/economie/2012/04/16/jim-yong-kim-nouveau-president-de-la-banque-mondiale_812101>.

L'Express, "Kofi Annan répond aux critiques dont l'ONU fait l'objet. "*l'Express, RFI, TV5*, 10 Jan. 2014. <http://www.lexpress.fr/info/monde/dossier/onu/dossier.asp?ida=43492

Index

www.ingramcontent.com/pod-product-compliance
Lightning Source LLC
Chambersburg PA
CBHW021433170526
45164CB00001B/227